"Dr. Steinbron has done it again! In this excellent book he refreshes and informs us about enabling the laity to provide pastoral care to the congregation. We have used the Lay Pastors Ministry here at Frazer Memorial with tremendous results for more than five years. It works! And it works because it is biblical."

DR. JOHN ED MATHISON

Senior Minister, Frazer Memorial United Methodist Church
Montgomery, Alabama

"Theoreticians are good. Practitioners are better. Mel Steinbron is both. His thinking is crystal-clear. And he has 'lived out' his theology of the laity in a way few have. All of us have limited time, limited resources; thus we must limit our reading to books that will really make a difference! This is definitely one of them."

DR. JIM GARLOW

Senior Pastor, Skyline Wesleyan Church
Lemon Grove, California

"The contagious churches of the next century will be very different from traditional churches today. One revolutionary difference will revolve around pastoral care. *Everyone* will receive regular pastoral care—from a gifted and trained *layperson!* This book will catalyze and inform this movement in thousands of congregations."

GEORGE G. HUNTER

Dean, School of World Mission and Evangelism
Asbury Theological Seminary, Wilmore, Kentucky
Author of *How to Reach Secular People* and
Church for the Unchurched

"I've always believed in the theory of liberating lay people to do ministry in the local church. In *The Lay-Driven Church*, Mel Steinbron converts theory to fact. Using biblical principles, he offers practical ways to make it happen. This book offers encouragement to pastors and laypeople alike."

REV. DR. ROBERT W. DICKSON

Pastor Emeritus, Hope Presbyterian Church
Richfield, Minnesota

"I have seen the fruit of Mel Steinbron's ministry for more than 20 years. It is choice! He not only preaches 'equipping the laity,' he practices it. This book is an excellent tool for pastors who want to share their ministries, and for laypersons who desire to serve in ministry. Mel writes from personal experience and most importantly from his pastor's heart! The biblical principles he expounds are working in small rural churches and in large urban churches. It will work in yours."

DR. RON RAND
Founder and President, UpBuilding Ministries
Former staff colleague with Mel Steinbron

"*The Lay-Driven Church* is a good and helpful book. It will encourage pastors and churches to equip and partner with laypeople in the crucial ministry of pastoral care."

REV. SIANG-YANG TAN, PH.D.
Associate Professor of Psychology
Fuller Theological Seminary, Pasadena, California
and Senior Pastor of First Evangelical Church
Glendale, California

"One of God's key strategies for effective ministry is multiplication. This biblical and practical book will help you multiply ministry...and release the power of the church as God intended. Pastors doing all the ministry is an unbiblical approach that churches in this age can no longer afford. *The Lay-Driven Church* is about releasing energy for ministry. Your investment in reading this book and practicing what it preaches will return dividends that release your church to be the Church."

KENT R. HUNTER
Creative Consultation Services, Corunna, Indiana

"During his 19 years directing lay pastoral ministry, Dr. Steinbron has demonstrated a wonderful blending of spiritual vitality with practical know-how. This book lets you into his very heart where that passion and practice originate. His walk with Jesus comes through clearly as he teaches. This is an inspiring volume for both church leaders and lay pastoral-care givers."

DR. NILS C. FRIBERG
Professor of Pastoral Care
Bethel Theological Seminary, St. Paul, Minnesota

The Lay-Driven Church

Dr. Melvin J. Steinbron

FOUNDER OF THE LAY PASTORS MINISTRY
AUTHOR OF *CAN THE PASTOR DO IT ALONE?*

Wipf & Stock
PUBLISHERS
Eugene, Oregon

Wipf and Stock Publishers
199 W 8th Ave, Suite 3
Eugene, OR 97401

The Lay-Driven Church
By Steinbron, Melvin J.
Copyright©1997 by Steinbron, Melvin J.
ISBN: 1-59752-021-7
Publication date 12/16/2004
Previously published by Regal Books, 1997

Dedication

To Char, my wife of five-plus decades.
I call her Honey.
I also call her my Silent Partner because
her support is the quiet, low-profile kind,
just the type God knew I needed for my life,
my ministry and for writing this book.

Contents

```
PART I:
What Kind of Church
Does It Take?
```

```
┌─────────────────────────────────┐
│           PART II:              │
│      What Kind of People        │
│          Does It Take?          │
└─────────────────────────────────┘
```

```
┌─────────────────────────────────┐
│           PART III:             │
│      What Kind of Effort        │
│          Does It Take?          │
└─────────────────────────────────┘
```

Acknowledgments

Scores of laypeople in all the churches where I have served throughout the past years have had a part in writing this book. They are my brothers and sisters in Christ and in ministry. I learned from them while they were learning from me. They mentored me while I mentored them. We grew together while discovering how to be partners in ministry.

I have fond memories and great respect for the people in the churches where I have served:

First Presbyterian, Ellsworth, Wisconsin;
Westminster Presbyterian, Duluth, Minnesota;
Haili Congregational, Hilo, Hawaii;
Randolph Heights Presbyterian, St. Paul, Minnesota;
College Hill Presbyterian, Cincinnati, Ohio;
Hope Presbyterian, Richfield, Minnesota.

Other significant people who have had a part in writing this book are the committed and competent laypeople in churches of many denominations in the United States, Canada, Australia and the Bahamas where I have conducted seminars. Also, the 25 clergy and laypeople who have been with me in pioneering what has become Lay Pastors Ministry, Inc. Each one knows of whom I speak, and I know them. We have become "family."

To God be the glory! Nehemiah said, "My God put it into my heart to assemble the...people" (7:5). I applied that great security to myself during the months of writing. "My God put it in my heart to write this book." I truly believe He did.

Introduction

"How long does it take to write a book?" I'm asked this question often.

My best answer is, "Nearly two decades."

What you are about to read comes from my steady involvement with the Lay Pastors Ministry. It originated in our church in 1978 to care for our 2,000-plus members, then it spread regionally as other churches adopted or adapted this model. Next, it spread nationally and internationally through my first book, *Can the Pastor Do It Alone?*[1]

In my part-time position on the pastoral staff of Hope Presbyterian Church in Richfield, Minnesota, I continue to have a hands-on experience with the Lay Pastors Ministry. Every day I know again the "agony and ecstasy" of ministry in action. My position as founder of the Lay Pastors Ministry and president of Lay Pastors Ministry, Inc., keeps me aware of other churches starting, managing and sometimes restarting or burying their ministries. I have been invited to give seminars in churches of 26 denominations (and many nondenominational churches) in the United States, Canada, Australia and the Bahamas.

Revelation 2:7 reads: "He who has an ear, let him hear what the Spirit says to the churches." Increasing numbers of churches are hearing the Spirit, which explains why this ministry continues to grow. The Lay Pastors Ministry is one of the new things God is doing in His Church. It has found its niche in the "Second Reformation," having proved its lasting value by being a usable model for congregational care.

A persistent part of my self-talk while writing this book was, *Mel, who are you writing for?* The question kept me focused. Nearly two decades of my pastoral years have been devoted to equipping churches and their people for lay pastoral ministry, so I could have chosen many different themes. However, I am writing this book for people committed to the idea of lay ministry.

This book is practicable. Knowing that *theology* without *doing* is fruitless, and *doing* without *theology* is pointless, I have strived to maintain a balance between principle and practice. Many excellent books are available about the theology and theory of lay ministry, but not many deal with its application. What is usually missing is how to get from where the reader is to where he or she wants to be—how to move from vision to reality.

Vocational and volunteer ministers who want to start a lay ministry, and those who want to maintain an existing healthy ministry will, in this book, discover the steps they need to take. So will those who want to renew, rebuild or reinspire a declining ministry. For some chapters, I have included laboratory experiences, called "Labs," in the appendix. They can be used by individuals, groups or in training sessions.

The focus for this book is lifted almost verbatim from Romans 12:6-8. The cadence in the *New International Version* uses the refrain "Let him" after each of the seven ministry gifts, concluding with "Let him do it." Hence the powerful, revolutionary, newly discovered dynamics for "The Next Church,"[2] *Let laypeople do it!*

The centerpiece of this book is the Lay Pastors Ministry, a system of congregational care by laypeople. Pastoral care is traditionally clergy turf. Now, however, this very important ministry is being given to the people. I see pastoral care by laypeople as decentralization. Moses provided an example. Taking the wise counsel of Jethro, he decentralized the care of Israel by reducing it to caring size—10 people per leader (see Exod. 18).

Even though my model is the Lay Pastors Ministry, the same fundamental principles undergird lay ministries of all kinds. The biblical call in Ephesians 4:11,12 is to be heard by *all* Christians in *all* churches for *all* ministries:

> It was he who gave some to be apostles, some to be
> prophets, some to be evangelists, and some to be pastors

and teachers, to prepare God's people for works of service, so that the body of Christ may be built up.

Pastors, church leaders, denominational heads, seminary professors and "ordinary people" will find this book to be a reservoir of tried-and-true principles, usable ideas, plans, suggestions, biblical teachings and helps of all kinds. You should be able to find yourself in the following list:

1. Pastors and/or lay leaders concerned about the care of their members and searching for a working model;
2. Churches that have a lay pastoral care ministry and see the need to "beef it up";
3. Pastors and church officers who want to raise the "one another" caring level of their congregations;
4. Seminary professors, particularly those in the pastoral care departments;
5. Pastors who want to ignite their people with a vision for authentic and effective lay ministry;
6. Small Group leaders or administrators looking for training and encouragement in caring for the members of their groups;
7. Sunday School or Adult Bible Class ("Learning Communities" is what we call ours) leaders and teachers desiring help in caring for the individual members of their classes;
8. People who want vital up-to-date information about what is happening in today's church regarding lay ministry;
9. "Ordinary people" who want to use their spiritual gifts in ministry;
10. Continuing education or Doctor of Ministry candidates working on studies, papers or projects in any area of lay ministry.

The central pastoral activity of a lay pastor lies in the acronym P A C E. It is important to keep this acronym in mind. Whenever you read about the Lay Pastors Ministry in the following pages, you will need to think P A C E to get the picture.

P: Lay pastors PRAY regularly for the members of their 5 to 10 households.

A: Lay pastors are AVAILABLE to their people in times of need and celebration.

C: Lay pastors CONTACT their people regularly, a minimum of once a month.

E: Lay pastors strive to be the best EXAMPLE they can be— not perfect, but moving in that direction.

In a way, this book serves as an update on what has happened to the Lay Pastors Ministry since the publication of my first book in 1987. But more than that, it moves beyond my first book. Significant discoveries during these years have brought this ministry to new heights of effectiveness and longevity. Some discoveries are:

1. The Lay Pastors Ministry works. It does what it is supposed to do.

2. As with anything that is alive, adjustments and adaptations have to be made. Changes based on experience, new insights, evaluation and trial-and-error are necessary.

3. Prayer is absolutely essential! Jesus said, "Apart from me you can do nothing" (John 15:5). It's true!

4. There is a genius in P A C E, which is a complete operational description of adequate pastoral care.

5. "Twelve Foundation Blocks" undergird the ministry. If any one of them begins to weaken, the whole ministry is at risk. These are fleshed out in chapter 7.

6. The ministry works in churches of all sizes. It is found in 49 states in the United States, 6 provinces in Canada, 5 states in Australia, the Bahamas, South Africa and other countries.

7. The ministry is adaptable to particular church needs and people. We have urged churches to use the principles in adopting or adapting the structure. No two churches do it exactly the same; some are creatively different.

8. Ministries that fail, usually fail for specific reasons.

9. Some churches move on to other forms of caring for their people, having cut their teeth on the Lay Pastors Ministry.

10. Many of the ministry's problems are common to all church-es. The two most common are recruiting and motivating.

11. Churches need to position their lay pastoral care min-istries into their total programs.

12. The "culture" of each church determines the need, priori-ty and viability of its ministries.

13. Love is the essence of this ministry. Without love, pastoral care is "only a resounding gong or a clanging cymbal" (1 Cor. 13:1).

14. The ministry is as good as the people doing it.

These discoveries are the makings of this book. It will therefore be a continuing useful resource to those who already have a lay pastoral care ministry, to those who are contemplating the possibilities and to those who are starting other lay ministries or have them on-line.

My two books *Can the Pastor Do It Alone?* and this one have some-thing in common with two pictures that hang close together in our home. Each by itself is complete. When viewed together as one, how-ever, a synergistic principle is at work—their combined beauty exceeds the loveliness of their separate scenes.

Each of these two books is a complete message. Each stands alone and is not dependent upon the other. When you read both of them, however, you activate a synergistic energy that creates a value larger than the sum of their separate messages. In brief, you don't need both books, but much is to be gained by having both.

For example, in *Can the Pastor Do It Alone?*, the description of the Lay Pastors Ministry and the steps required to start it are given. But...the description and steps assume that the pastor and congrega-tion are ready for it. What if they aren't?

This book furnishes the theology and methodology to prepare the people and/or a church not only to start, but also to sustain this min-istry. The synergistic value is that you can now implement a lay pas-toral care ministry that will be effective and endure because you have all that is needed: the plan, the people and a church culture that is favorable to it. And, the principles which work for a lay pastoral care ministry will work as well for all lay ministries.

While writing this book, I struggled with the words "lay" and "cler-gy." Sometimes I will substitute "volunteer minister" for "lay" and "vocational minister" for "clergy." Using "lay" and "clergy" perpetuates an unbiblical dichotomy, but I usually bow to those words because they are the common verbal currency. My substitutions are more accurate, but also more clumsy. Loren Mead, founder of the Alban Institute, says we don't even have terminology to talk about what is happening in the Church today. He is right!

Before we continue, I invite you to share your ideas, insights and ministry experiences with me. If you are finding additional and better principles, ideas and forms, please let me hear from you. You can play a significant part in helping other churches by telling us your story. We, Lay Pastors Ministry, Inc. (LPMI),[3] are committed to servicing churches with the best material available through our quarterly *Network News*, monographs, videotapes, seminars and conferences. Some of the best will come from you.

Notes

1. Melvin J. Steinbron, *Can the Pastor Do It Alone?* (Ventura, Calif.: Regal Books, 1987).
2. "The Next Church" is the intriguing title of an article by Charles Trueheart in the August 1996 issue of *The Atlantic Monthly*. Hints of the content are given in these sentences: "Centuries of European tradition and Christian habit are deliberately being abandoned, clearing the way for new contemporary forms of worship and belonging"; and "The Next Church movement makes many traditional church leaders, and many active Christians nervous, because it implies rejection of the tried and once-true and the somehow holy..." pp. 37-38.
3. Lay Pastors Ministry, Inc., 7132 Portland Ave. S., Minneapolis, MN 55423. Phone: (612) 866-4055 or (612) 423-2449. Fax: (612) 866-8226 or (612) 423-9245.

PART I:
What Kind of Church Does It Take?

A Needs-Conscious Church

The denomination didn't make any difference to this man—neither did the location nor the size. The preaching and music, though important, were not first on his list. He was searching for a church where people were real in their relationships. For several Sundays following the close of the service, he stood at the edge of the milling crowd, critically observing the way people related to each other.

He had been burned in his former church. The relationships were superficial. People were cordial, even polite. They smiled and nodded their heads as they greeted one another, but it was evident they were hurrying to more important agendas. He had thought people cared, but when the chips were down, no one was there for him. No one really cared.

In *this* church, however, he sensed a different culture. People were real. He saw them taking time to talk. Their smiles and gestures signaled bonded relationships. He eavesdropped just enough to conclude that people were really interested in one another's lives—their families and jobs, their troubles and sorrows, their joys and excitements. He saw one cry. He watched another throw her head back in laughter. He even observed a small group in the corner join hands in prayer.

After a few Sundays, he ventured inward from the fringe to see if he would be accepted. People talked with him. They included him in their little circles. Upon discovering that he was a visitor, one person offered to walk him to the refreshment table, then to the Information Center.

This was a different church culture. People were real. He was accepted. He was sure his new acquaintances truly cared. Before long he attended classes, reaffirmed his faith in Jesus Christ and joined the church.

Now that he's "in" what will happen? Will the momentum of this church's culture move him into doing a ministry as it moved him into membership? Are there *Discover Your Ministry* paths to follow with people who will accompany him through the process, like the person who walked him to the refreshment table? Is lay ministry as characteristic of the culture of the church as the love and care he is experiencing?

> If a church is to be all God calls it to be, it will also respond to the *unfelt needs* of its people.

The church responded to his *felt needs* for love and acceptance. But if a church is to be all God calls it to be, it will also respond to the *unfelt needs* of its people by: One, learning what the Bible teaches about spiritual gifts, and two, equipping people to use those gifts.

Children's unfelt needs illustrate this. A child psychologist, being interviewed on a TV talk show, explained that children do not come to their parents complaining that their parents are not spending enough time with them. They do not ask for more quality time so they can develop into well-rounded adults. But parents who are alert to their children's behavioral symptoms will see that is what they need.

So it is with pastoral care in a church. Many people struggle and suffer with their problems alone, having no idea that they need pastoral care. It is a rare person who will come to the pastor to request more personal attention. But an alert pastor will pick up on clues such as sporadic attendance; arrested spiritual growth; minimal participation in the life of the church; and criticism of sermons, programs and people.

This is a new day in the Church. Leaders clinging to the traditional way of "doing" church are struggling. Many churches are in a survival mode. A six-month study conducted throughout the first part of 1996 indicated that congregations find themselves stuck in old patterns that seem preoccupied with institutional maintenance. Many, however, are moving or have moved from the traditional to the new and are bursting with life.

Loren Mead, the perceptive founder of the Alban Institute, strongly believes the Church has to be "reinvented." He maintains the changes needed are so major that instead of tampering with congregations or polishing them up a bit, we need to "reinvent" them.[1] Management consultant Peter Drucker also believes churches are in trouble. Those that will not only survive into the next century but thrive are those which are *"pastoral."* He defines *pastoral* as giving attention to the needs of people.[2]

A panoramic sweep of Church history indicates we are in an interim age, uncertain whether we are to hold on to the past or take strident steps into the future. One thing is for sure: The Church can't stay where it is. Traditional structures are collapsing; membership and finances are declining. Our culture, in general, is indifferent, hostile or benignly tolerant. It does not take the Church seriously, and is not supportive.

In this interim age (the period between what the Church was and what it is becoming), church-development strategies differ significantly. Some churches are trying to recapture the past. Their goal is: Do what we did before, only bigger and better. Some are holding steady. Their hope is: The curve somehow will soon turn upward. Others are shifting gears. Their risk is: We'll cast our lot with the Scriptures and successful church models.

One of the dominant characteristics of churches bursting with life is lay ministry. They are giving the ministry to the people. They are calling their people to commit themselves to the lordship of Jesus Christ, to spiritual growth and to ministry. They help their people discover their gifts for ministry and equip them to do it. They support them in what they believe God is calling them to do, and hold them accountable. They believe that all Christians are ministers (some vocational and some volunteer), equal in importance while different in function. They believe the laity should be the primary ministering people in the Church.

The genre of lay ministry we are presenting in this book is pastoral care. The model we feature is the Lay Pastors Ministry, a system of congregational care by laypeople. The history of the Lay Pastors Ministry (nearly two decades now) warrants the focus. The model launched in one church in 1978, with no thought that it would go anywhere else, has been adopted and adapted by hundreds of other churches around the world.

Pastors who discover that they cannot give every member the kind of care they need are relieved to discover this successful system. They often say, "This will keep us from having to reinvent the wheel." Informed laypeople, concerned about the exodus out the "back door" (or "disaffiliation"), become excited over the possibility of the Lay Pastors Ministry closing that door. Churches that put a priority on pastoral care look to us to help them implement this ministry, or, as many have done, just start it themselves by following the principles and plan given in my first book, *Can the Pastor Do It Alone?*

In this book I ask and then answer four key questions:

1. Are people ready to give and receive this ministry?
2. Are pastors ready to give this ministry to their people?
3. Are people ready to do this ministry?
4. What kind of structure does this ministry take?

The last three chapters cite reasons why laypeople can do this ministry, ways they can do it, how to give the ministry to the people and how lay pastoral care fits into your church's total life.

My prayer is that as you read and ponder what is written, you shall hear the refrain of Revelation 2:7 regularly: "He who has an ear, let him hear what the Spirit says to the churches." This same refrain concludes the message to each of the seven churches (see 2:7,11,17,29; 3:6,13,22).

Be prepared to read this refrain at the conclusion of each chapter because I believe present-day indicators signal that the Spirit "says" the message of this book to your church.

Also, just as each church's message ended with a specific directive from the Spirit, each of these chapters ends with a specific directive.

The success of your church's lay pastoral care ministry will be in proportion to its energy for these seven qualities:

- A Needs-Conscious Church
- A Gift-Oriented Church
- An Egalitarian Church
- A Ministry-Balanced Church
- A Biblical Church
- A Mobilized Church
- A Failure-Resistant Church.

Each quality warrants full treatment, therefore, I have written a chapter about each one.

So let's consider in this chapter what it means to be a needs-conscious church.

ALERT TO THE NEED FOR PASTORAL CARE

To have a successful lay pastoral care ministry, the church must be needs-conscious: alert to the needs of its people for pastoral care and ready to (1) *assess* the need; (2) *adapt* to changing realities; (3) *adopt* or create a structure; and (4) *advance* with specific plans, goals and personnel.

Ready to Assess the Need

For several years, I have presented pastoral care seminars in churches that have established pastoral care as a priority. This priority usually results from a survey or other kind of study. Often the needs assessment is generated by a frustrated pastor, fueled by disillusioned members and is conducted by a board or assigned group.

Gary Titusdahl's story is the same as that of hundreds of churches. Gary is the pastor of a growing church, The First Congregational Church (UCC) in Cannon Falls, Minnesota.[3]

> It became clear to me that I could not provide quality pastoral care alone....I felt guilty....I also felt inadequate as a pastoral caregiver for the entire congregation.
>
> The church's annual evaluation of my performance in 1992 described my pastoral care efforts as appreciated and, for the most part, effective. But, the congregation wanted more attention paid to its ongoing pastoral needs. In particular, the congregation said it needed more

thorough follow-up to individuals and families suffering loss, confusion and grief.

Group meetings were scheduled in members' homes throughout a period of several weeks so people could voice their opinions. Pastoral care was overwhelmingly determined to be the number one need.

But Gary was already on overload, thus it became clear that if members were to be adequately pastored, laypeople would have to do it. Enter the Lay Pastors Ministry.

I was invited to lead their first equipping seminar. Sunday, January 22, 1995, was a historic day—the first members were commissioned as lay pastors. People were excited, and their expectations were high.

The following week they began to P A C E their assigned flocks of five to eight households. Remember P A C E? This constituted their pastoral care:

P: PRAYING regularly for them;
A: Being AVAILABLE to them;
C: CONTACTING them; and
E: Striving to be an EXAMPLE.

Four typical dynamics are apparent in Gary's story:

1. Only one pastoral caregiver: "I could not provide quality pastoral care alone."
2. Feelings of guilt and inadequacy: "I felt guilty...inadequate."
3. Involving people in needs assessment: "They scheduled meetings in members' homes."
4. Pastoral care identified as the priority: "They felt the urgency to develop a systematic approach to pastoral care."

What did the people meeting in these homes mean by *pastoral care*? Obviously they did not mean spiritual leadership, preaching, marrying, burying, counseling and crisis visitation. Gary was doing these. Let's hear how they understood *lay pastoral care*:

• "More thorough follow-up to individuals and families suffering loss, confusion and grief."

- "Responsive means to provide spiritual care for the width and depth of [people's] pain."
- "Giving personal attention, support and guidance in Christ's name."
- "Carry others' burdens and spur one another on toward love and good deeds."

People joining our churches deserve the kind of personal attention described in the words you have just read; and clearly, if they are going to receive it, laypeople must give it. The centerpiece of the Lay Pastors Ministry, P A C E, adequately provides this one-on-one, "love-with-skin-on-it" kind of pastoral care.

Formal assessment of the need for pastoral care by involving the congregation does three things: (1) It brings people in on the ground floor of a new system. Being involved in the process makes their "ownership" likely. (2) The solid data gathered in the meetings helps the leaders of the congregation make informed and firm decisions. (3) It assures acceptance, both by those who will become lay pastors and members who are to receive their care.

Ready to Adapt to Changing Realities

For some reason churches are more resistant to change than other federations of people. All religion has a tendency to fossilize. No change means death; radical and sudden change can also mean death. Balance between the two extremes is the key to healthy change.

Some things in the church should never change; some things are changeable and need to be changed; other things change without our choice. As we apply these three realities to pastoral care we see: First, the need for care never changes. Second, the kinds of need and the ways of caring change. Third, our high-tech, increasingly impersonal, life-in-the-fast-lane culture has forced changes upon us, setting our agenda for us—giving personal care on a continuing basis.

The kind of church ready for this ministry will adapt to changing realities.

Ready to Adopt or Create a Structure

To move from assessing the need to meeting the need, a church must adopt (or create) a structure. It will search for a visible form within which the invisible dynamics can come alive.

How often a survey has led to nothing more than a file cabinet drawer filled with responses to questions; talk about what should be done has been nothing more than that—talk. Somehow, someone has to carry the data and intention forward.

Many churches have done what the First Congregational Church (UCC) of Cannon Falls, Minnesota, did: appoint a task force of a few committed people to search for the best model of lay pastoral care available to them. After considering others, they selected the Lay Pastors Ministry. Other churches opt for different models. Some invent their own, taking principles and parts from existing packaged-and-ready-to-go ministries.

In 1987, Earl Andrews, the minister of congregational care for Frazer Memorial United Methodist Church in Montgomery, Alabama,

> **A ministry launched without specific plans, goals and a "point person" is destined to mediocrity at best and failure at worst.**

read my book *Can the Pastor Do It Alone?* (Regal Books), while flying home from Israel. He mused, *This will keep us from having to reinvent the wheel.* His congregation has 7,000 members to care for. I was invited to present our model of lay pastoral care to a select group of members who adopted our model. Later, they made necessary adaptations to their particular context.

Amazing! On the very day I was writing these words about adopting a structure, I received this fax from Ed Marshall, pastor of the Durbanville Baptist Church in Durbanville, South Africa:

> Greetings from South Africa. Since last speaking with you in October 1994, we have decided to implement the lay pastor program in our church. The delay has been caused by...having to build to accommodate a growing congregation.

He then proceeded to ask about resources that would help them.

Adopting or creating an adequate form for the pastoral care ministry idea can be likened to birthing a child. If there is to be a child, the idea must move from desire and intention through conception and gestation to the delivery of a visible body. The point is made. The church in which this ministry can happen is a church ready to adopt, adapt or create a structure for the ministry.

Ready to Advance with Specific Plans, Goals and a "Point Person"

Can you imagine a basketball team going into a game without a game plan? Can you imagine an investor transferring money without setting a goal for its performance? Can you imagine a group of entrepreneurs starting a business without providing a "point person"—the one whose desk sign reads, "The buck stops here!"?

A ministry launched without specific plans, goals and a "point person" is destined to mediocrity at best and failure at worst. The people putting the ministry together must finalize the plans and get them on paper like an architect does for a house. Vague, undefined plans weaken a ministry from the start and open the door for misunderstanding and failure. Goals have to be set so workers have something against which to evaluate the effectiveness of the ministry and make "in-flight" corrections. A "point person," whether volunteer or salaried, is mandatory. Somebody has to be in charge.

Two flourishing models demonstrate ways to *assess* the need, *adapt* to changing realities, *adopt* or create a structure and *advance* with specific plans, goals and personnel. The first is the Eastridge Park Christian Church in Mesquite, Texas. In a 15-year period, the congregation grew from 300 to 2,000 members. If they were to do right by their people and be true to Christ's calling to "take care of my sheep" (John 21:16), they knew they had to do things differently. Senior minister Dan H. Carroll wrote:

> By the mid-1980s, we began facing more and more challenging tasks as we attempted to minister to [the congregation's] individual needs and provide...a nurturing church home. Clearly more of this work surfaced than the ministers could do effectively.[4]

They believed that the call to ministry extends to all Christians, not just to ordained clergy. "We are all shepherds," he stressed. To achieve their goal, "to minister to its members in areas of lay pastoral care," they created a near carbon copy of what the church in Cannon Falls, Minnesota did, even though the membership difference was 270 compared to 2,000. What they titled, "Four Essentials for an Effective Church," assured their success:

1. Listen to people's deepest yearnings.
2. Put together a system that will meet people's basic expectations of the church.
3. Improve the system so it goes beyond people's expectations to delight and excite them.
4. Act [through leaders] to empower all the people to contribute to the effort.

Even though Eastridge Park came up with a model quite different from our Lay Pastors Ministry, their "Cluster Program" accomplished the same objective. It enabled members to minister to one

> The biblical way to operate the church is on the basis of spiritual gifts.

another. These words from the pastor are encouraging to every church leader aware of needing a structured pastoral care program for the congregation: "You don't need a complicated planning process, but you have to do some basic things." By "basic things" Pastor Carroll meant the four essentials listed previously: assess, adapt, adopt and advance.

- **Assess:** The congregation experienced more pastoral care needs than the paid staff could attend to.
- **Adapt:** Acknowledge that people who are not getting their

needs met will move on. Loyalties to the organization do not exist.

- **Adopt:** They created the Cluster Program, a decentralized plan within which members ministered to one another.
- **Advance:** They moved from need through planning to implementation.

The second model is Christ Church in Fort Lauderdale, Florida.[5] As Pastor Dick Willis tells it, his personal new awakening, which was deeply spiritual and born of the Holy Spirit, launched the church into a lay pastoral care ministry. In addition to surrendering his life to God, he needed to surrender the control of the ministries in the church to the laity.

He said he had to unlearn much of what he was taught in seminary. Instead of being a "professional minister," he saw his responsibility now to spiritually feed and equip laity to do the ministries of Christ Church. The biblical way to operate the church is on the basis of spiritual gifts. In this way, each person finds a place of ministry.

In June of 1994, Pastor Willis began to consecrate lay pastors. By April 1995, 80 had been appointed. Three categories of lay pastors comprise their model: (1) Wesley Group leaders (the goal is 400 of these groups meeting weekly); (2) Administrative Groups, such as trustees; and (3) Action Ministries, such as ushers and prison ministry. Each group has a lay pastor, the basic care-giving person in the congregation for his or her group.

This model demonstrates the same four essentials:

- **Assess:** First, a personal assessment led to spiritual and ministry renewal. Second, they learned that 80 percent of the 1.4 million people in Broward County are unchurched.
- **Adapt:** His "new awakening" reoriented his life as a minister. Surrendering control of the ministries to the laity reoriented the people.
- **Adopt:** The church is perceived to have three categories of lay pastors. A plan was established for leading and staffing the various groups of laity.
- **Advance:** A person who feels called to be a lay pastor meets with one of the ordained pastors. If the call fits the church's vision, that person is invited to be a lay pastor.

Part of being alert to the need for pastoral care is to be aware of and concerned about *all* members. It's not unlike parents of a large family who must be equally aware of and concerned for each child, the prodigal as well as the bonded. Joining a church is a two-way commitment: new members commit to active participation while the church commits to nurturing and caring for them.

Too often, when a member's commitment lessens, the church is not alert to the signals, doesn't care or does not have a ministry plan for reaching out to these people. A study made by a denominational leader, *Why They Left Their Church*,[6] identified two major reasons people leave: failed expectations and broken or undeveloped relationships. The *coup de grâce* was failure of others in the congregation to miss them after they had withdrawn.

> Two-thirds of those interviewed said they received no contact of any kind inquiring about their absence after they quit attending. Nearly half indicated they would have welcomed a meaningful inquiry from the pastor, or other church leader, and that it could have made a difference in their decision to disaffiliate.
>
> A mother...said, "We had a daughter with a fatal disease....From June until her death in November, we had heard not one word from the minister."
>
> "I felt very abandoned in my church. I just don't feel connected anymore as a person. I don't think my presence makes any difference in that church."

The process of disaffiliating begins with a *Discomfort Stage*, moves to a *Withdrawing Stage* and culminates in the *Exiting Stage*. The best time to prevent dropout is prior to or during the *Discomfort Stage*. The most effective antidote for reaching those in the *Discomfort Stage* is to provide a climate for lively interaction with others in the congregation and to create a formal caring network.

This will not happen by itself. Neither will it happen if it is left to the pastoral staff—not because they are under committed or lack ambition, but because they are already overloaded with priority ministries. It can, however, happen when a church wants it enough to plan intentionally for it, using as its starting point the awareness of the need for pastoral care—a needs-conscious church.

"He who has an ear, let him hear what the Spirit says to the church-es." Be alert to your church's pastoral care needs.

Notes

1. Loren Mead, *Action Information* (May/June 1990) published by The Alban Institute, 4125 Nebraska Ave., N.W., Washington, D.C. 20016.
2. Peter F. Drucker, *The New Realities* (New York, N.Y.: Harper & Row, 1989), p. 200.
3. Gary A. Titusdahl, "The Lay Pastors Ministry," a thesis project dissertation, Doctor of Ministry Program, Cannon Falls, Minnesota. This document is at the library of United Theological Seminary of the Twin Cities, 3000 Fifth Street, N.W., New Brighten, MN, 55112, Phone: 612-633-4311.
4. *Net Results* (June 1994), published monthly by the National Evangelistic Association of the Christian Church.
5. *Circuit Rider* (April 1994), a publication of the United Methodist Church, 9-11.
6. *Presbyterian Life and Times* (October 1992), published by the Synod of Lakes and Prairies, Bloomington, MN 55425.

A Gift-Oriented Church

"NOW ABOUT SPIRITUAL GIFTS..."

The new pastor spent all day unpacking books, visiting in hospitals and contacting some of the church leaders. The hour came for the annual church dinner, which had been planned long before his arrival. He was fatigued and famished. He stood in line along with other people, visiting and slowly moving toward the food. Looking up ahead, he noticed a woman forking one piece of chicken onto each plate. Before long he was at that spot.

Because he was hungry he asked for two pieces. The reply: "One piece to each person. Please move along."

The pastor looked at her and said, "I've had no time to eat since breakfast. Please, could I have two pieces?"

Her firm answer surprised him: "Each one gets just one piece. Please move along."

He thought he would pull rank: "Perhaps you don't know who I am; I'm the new pastor of the church."

He was shocked by her even firmer response, "Perhaps you don't know who *I* am; I'm the lady in charge of chicken."

I told this story to a group of people in a new elder-orientation class. They laughed and I laughed with them. Then I asked them to read Romans 12:6-8 and explain the connection to the story. After reading the verses, they chuckled reverently. One volunteered, "I see the connection. If a woman's gift is forking out chicken, let her fork out chicken. Each person has a special gift for his or her ministry."

The kind of church in which lay ministry can be successful is the kind that will let laypeople use their gifts. A great variety of gifts is required because a great variety of ministries exists. The Holy Spirit orchestrates the giving and the using of spiritual gifts:

> All these are the work of one and the same Spirit, and he gives them to each one, just as he determines (1 Cor. 12:11).

Because the Spirit determines who gets what and who should do what, each of us needs to listen to the Spirit. Listening is a personal and private matter. It often happens, however, in a public place, or during an unexpected moment such as a worship service, a retreat, while conversing with a brother or sister in Christ or while observing or participating in a missions project. How to hear the Lord is a great mystery; but one thing is clear, all who wish to hear will hear.

A plethora of helpful books, tapes, manuals, magazine articles, along with several practical gifts-assessment tests have poured forth throughout the past three decades. Word is getting around that *every* Christian is endowed with spiritual gifts. The apostle Paul started it:

> Now about spiritual gifts, brothers [and sisters], I do not want you to be ignorant (1 Cor. 12:1).

I do not intend to add to the gifts literature. I just want to call your attention to spiritual gifts and add a few thoughts. One thought is that by combining two major teachings—the variety of gifts and the use of the gifts—we conclude that people cannot be randomly interchanged.

The traditional church elects or appoints people to ministry positions as though any willing person can take his or her turn at that task. Churches that have functioned this way for generations find it difficult to start matching people's tasks with their spiritual gifts. They may have been merely filling slots instead of helping people to discover their spiritual gifts and hear God's call to their specific ministries.

"The most important decision facing your church today is the decision to shift the focus of your church from the ministry of the clergy to the ministry of the laity," writes one of America's prominent laymen, Robert Slocum. The possibility for this shift lies in every-member giftedness, the fact that God has endowed every Christian with gifts to use in ministry.

Slocum persuasively pursues this theme throughout his book, *Maximize Your Ministry*.[1] His thesis starts in the preface with a question, "What kind of church will be effective in the next century?" With the keen mind of an atomic physicist (he worked in such high-tech fields as space exploration and laser systems), keyed to analytical exactness, he answers his own question:

> I am convinced the effective church for the twenty-first century will be the church that mobilizes, equips, empowers and supports ordinary Christians in ministry.[2]

Bingo! The possibility for this lies in every-member giftedness.

Robert Slocum lays the responsibility for doing ministry on laypeople when he writes: "The challenge for each of us is to search out and identify our own call to lay ministry."[3] The search will be rewarded because God has already given every searcher his or her gifts for ministry. Slocum brilliantly assures each Christian a successful search: "The Early Church had a commissioning service for lay ministry; it was called baptism."[4]

The Scriptures are the source for such thinking. Romans 12:6-8 powerfully declares this truth. The words of this passage not only inspired the theme of this book, but also played a significant role in shaping my beliefs about lay ministry. I like the cadence of the *New International Version* (Steinbron paraphrase):

> If a man's[5] gift is prophesying, let him prophesy;
> If it is serving, let him serve;
> If is teaching, let him teach;
> If it is encouraging, let him encourage;
> If it is contributing, let him contribute;
> If it is leadership, let him lead;
> If it is showing mercy, let him show mercy.

These words sound like a mandate. They do not make ministry an option for us Christians. In our culture, people are not accustomed to accepting mandates. But this is not for people in our culture, it is for those who have been born anew into the culture of the kingdom of God. Mandates from God are an integral part of Kingdom culture.

"If it is encouraging, *let* him encourage!" (v. 8). *Let* is an imperative, therefore we need to know "who" is to *let*? Because *encouraging* is one of the pastoral gifts, we are talking about *letting* someone pastor. *Let laypeople do it!* Just who is to *let*?

THREE POSSIBLE ANSWERS...

1. You

You *let* means "*You* go ahead and do it. What are *you* waiting for?" If *you* are the one with the gift, *you* are expected to use it. Robert Slocum unequivocally insists that the responsibility for discovering ministry gifts and using them in service is the layperson's! This is true even for laypeople whose churches are not yet promoting lay ministry.[6] *You* are the one who is to *let*. It is as though the verse reads, "If your gift is encouraging, then by all means *you* encourage!" Or as Bill Hybels, pastor of Willow Creek Community Church in South Barrington, Illinois, would say it, "Men and women, if you've been given the gift of encouraging, for *God's sake,* encourage."[7]

2. Church Leaders

These are pastors, professional staff and other leaders. They need to step aside so people with gifts can minister, not just "help out." Each member of the church is to function in freedom and authority within the areas of his or her gifts. Because leaders by virtue of their positions are aware of *their* own ministries, the directive *let* means they are to recognize the ministries of *their* members as well. *Let* means they are to acknowledge people's giftedness, accept them as partners in ministry and affirm them in their roles.

To believe that laypeople are also authentic ministers in their own rights and to affirm the parity of ministries requires a major paradigm shift for most leaders of traditional churches. The shift is to solid ground because it is biblical. First Corinthians 12, for example, uses the human body to illustrate how all parts—prominent and hidden—are equally necessary.

Leaders, we dare not substitute preaching for action, or lip service for performance. *Let* is an active verb, suggesting that we must make a choice to allow. I am one who deceived himself for years, thinking that preaching it was doing it. I, along with a group of committed and competent laypeople, *let* by creating a structure for lay pastoral care and relinquishing the pastoral care ministry to equipped and commissioned laypeople.

3. The People

Again, our human body illustrates the truth that each part of the body needs every other part. "The eye cannot say to the hand, 'I don't need you!'" (1 Cor. 12:21). Let's apply this analogy to the Lay Pastors Ministry. Members cannot say to the lay pastor, "I don't need you!" The members of our churches are to *let* the lay pastors pastor them. They must let them into their homes and into their lives if the "body" is to function at its best. Conversely, the lay pastor will receive the ministry of those whose gifts are administration, prophecy or whatever. The mutual nature of all ministry is summarized in 1 Peter 4:10:

> Each one should use whatever gift he [or she] has received to serve others, faithfully administering God's grace in its various forms.

He who has an ear, let him hear what the Spirit says to the churches: If a man's gift is encouraging, let him encourage. If it is showing mercy, let him show mercy. You who have the gift, use it! You who are leaders, equip the saints, support them and step aside to let them use their gifts. You who are members, accept pastoral care from them.

People in my seminars often ask, "But isn't everybody supposed to care?" This is the reasoning of a traditional church-minded person. It is the proposed alternative to a structured Lay Pastors Ministry. The belief is that if everybody does their jobs, people will be cared for. But, this is the old and failed system of congregational care. Failure results from neglecting to distinguish between *caring in general* and *caring in particular*. *Caring in general* hasn't done it in the past, and it isn't going to be doing it in the future. There must be a better way—*caring in particular*.

Certainly, every Christian is to care for others, but not every Christian is given special gifts for pastoral care. This principle is also seen in other areas of church life. For example, every Christian is to witness for Christ, but not every Christian has the gift of evangelism (the gift of assisting an individual to personal faith in Jesus Christ as Savior and Lord). Every Christian is to give, but not every Christian has the gift of contributing (the gift of earning substantial sums of money in order to give large amounts to the church). Every Christian is to communicate some of what he or she knows about the Scriptures to family, friends and others, but not every Christian has the gift of teaching (the ability to formally instruct groups of people in the truths of God).

So, whereas every Christian is to care for others, not every Christian

> The *fruit* is essential for quality
> of life; the *gifts* are essential
> for ministry.

has the gift of *pastoring* (endowed with a spirit of mercy and the ability to encourage). A prime illustration of this is the Neighborhood Watch program: It is every citizen's job to watch for suspicious people; but the police are the specialists in crime prevention and criminal apprehension.

Whereas all members are to care for others, it is the layperson with pastoral gifts, training and commissioning who is the specialist in PACE-ing people.

The Scriptures make a clear distinction between the "fruit of the Spirit," which every Christian is to bear, and the "gifts of the Spirit," which are unique to each Christian. The *fruit* is essential for quality of life; the *gifts* are essential for ministry. Paul's analogy of the body with its many parts for special functions helps us understand *caring in particular.* The whole body is not an eye. The ear is not designed to sniff odors. The head and feet are each specialists in their unique functions.

This issue of caring in general versus caring in particular surfaced with high energy in one of my seminars. A participant challenged me from the floor: "We don't need a Lay Pastors Ministry. Everyone is a lay pastor! We just need to get our people to care for one another." My response was crucial because people from 23 churches were there seeking a way to care for their people.

I put four rhetorical questions to this person:

1. Is everyone in your church being prayed for regularly?
2. Does everyone have someone keeping in touch with him or her regularly?
3. Does everyone have someone to whom they can bare their soul, to whom they can comfortably turn when the chips are down?
4. Is it possible to get everyone to do his and her part?

After thanking the person for opening an important door for us, I addressed everyone...

> Take inventory by answering the following:
> How many members of your church are you *praying* for regularly? Does your pastor or any member pray specifically for you in your life situation daily or weekly?
> To how many of your members do you think you could be *available* in times of need or celebration? With how many have you built a relationship of trust so they will turn to you with confidence and ease?
> With how many are you in *contact* monthly (and meaningfully)?
> How many members know you well enough to see you as an *example*, not of a perfectly formed Christian, but one who loves the Lord, loves them and loves the church?

Recognize the italicized words as the ministry description for a lay pastor: P A C E. If pastoral care is to include all members and if it is to be done right, it takes people who have the pastoral gifts, who sense a call from God, who have been equipped and who give themselves to people within the structure designed to provide pastoral care for every member. They provide *care in particular* while others are providing (hit-and-miss) *care in general*.

To finish the story about the person who challenged the need for the intentional and structured pastoral care ministry, this person came to me after the seminar, apologized for her contrary spirit and emphatically affirmed that her church needed the *Lay Pastors Ministry*. She had just made what you call a paradigm shift, shifting from care in general to care in particular.

[
God has His part; we have our parts.
God provides the gifts to make
ministry possible; we provide the
bodies to do the ministry.
]

A slow but sure way for churches to make the paradigm shift, not only to care in particular, but also to the parity of all ministers (volunteer and vocational, the focus of the next chapter), is to inculcate the idea that God and all His people are in a ministry partnership. God has His part; we have our parts. God provides the gifts to make ministry possible; we provide the bodies to do the ministry. Five observations help us to understand this divine-human partnership:

- God provides the colors; we paint the pictures.
- God provides the notes; we write the music.
- God provides the soil; we plant the flowers.
- God provides the mind; we do the thinking.
- God provides the gifts; we do the ministry.

GOD'S PART

He provides the gifts. First Corinthians 12:11 teaches that spiritual gifts for ministry are given, not earned. They are not learned, not deserved and not initiated by us. They are not produced by seeking or desiring. They are not rewards for deep commitment and godly living. They are distributed to each person according to God's choosing. They are just there, waiting to be discovered and put to use.
He determines each person's unique gifts. Romans 12:6 informs us

that God gives different gifts according to His grace. *Grace* is the favor and generosity of God. First Corinthians 12:11 tells that the Spirit orchestrates the distribution of the gifts: "He gives them...just as he determines." They are not tossed like a bride's bouquet into the crowd; the Spirit deliberately assigns them.

He gives with the expectation that we will use them. First Peter 4:10 says it plainly: "Each one *should use* whatever gift he [or she] has received" (italics mine). Just as unused Christmas gifts presume poor choices, unused spiritual gifts seem to infer that God may have made some poor choices in His gift giving.

He gives with the intention that we will develop them. The fact that Scripture calls us to love God with our minds (see Luke 10:27), especially our renewed minds (see Rom. 12:2), suggests that we are to use our mental faculties to expand the use of our ministry gifts to their fullest dimensions. Peter's directive to "grow in the grace and knowledge of our Lord and Savior Jesus Christ" (see 2 Pet. 3:18) includes growth in the development of our ministry gifts.

My growth in using the word processor to provide this message for others illustrates the point. God gives the gifts; we are responsible for nourishing and nurturing them from their undeveloped beginnings to full-bodied potential, just as parents are responsible for nourishing and nurturing undeveloped infants to their full potentials.

YOUR PART

You provide the body. Romans 12, which lists seven gifts, starts with a call to offer your body as a living sacrifice to God. It is significant that Jesus gave His body: "this is my body given for you" (Luke 22:19). Romans 6:13 is specific: "Offer the parts of your body to him as instruments of righteousness." Name the parts:

- **Hands:** *Offer them* to help others;
- **Arms:** *Offer them* to comfort a struggling person;
- **Ears:** *Offer them* to hear another's anguish or joy;
- **Feet:** *Offer them* to run errands for an incapacitated person;
- **Eyes:** *Offer them* to read for a blind person;
- **Brain:** *Offer it* to create strategies for helping a person in

trouble or celebrating a person's festive occasion, such as an anniversary, graduation or birthday.

You provide the time. We won't get much done with our bodies if we use only discretionary time for ministry. If we want to use our bodies in partnership with God, we must build time for ministry into our schedules. For example, a lay pastor will have to intentionally schedule contacts by writing them on his or her calendar, or the body will never get around to it. This takes *self-control*, the ninth "fruit of the Spirit" (see Gal. 5).

You provide the skills. Just as the number and sharpness of tools the craftsman has to work with determines the quality of workmanship, so it is with ministry. Let's look at this example as it applies to the Lay Pastors Ministry. A lay pastor can begin to care for a small flock of people just by using whatever ability he or she now has. But that person needs to acquire additional skills to maximize the effectiveness of the spiritual gifts.

For example, if the gift is encouragement, the lay pastor may have an empathic spirit, but may not have all the listening skills required to hear the unspoken hurts as well as the words. Continual growth in skills enables us to be progressively better in ministry.

God's part and your part together make a whole. God is doing His part. When we do our part, His work gets done. God started the process by giving each of us gifts. Withholding our bodies, refusing to provide the time and failing to grow in skill stymies the process.

Many of us who are not withholding our bodies may, however, need the counsel Paul gave Timothy: "Do not neglect your gift" (1 Tim. 4:14); and, "Fan into flame the gift of God, which is in you" (2 Tim. 1:6). We can become careless and delinquent in doing our ministries, or we can become sloppy in our ways, settling for mediocrity. The flame can die down. Our enthusiasm for ministry is subject to entropy, a cooling effect that reduces the amount of energy available for ministry. If Timothy needed Paul's reminders not to neglect his gift, but to fan (or rekindle) his gift into flame, we Christians need the same reminders today.

The kind of church in which lay pastoral care can happen is the church that will *let* laypeople use their gifts. And if lay pastoral care is really going to happen, a structure such as the Lay Pastors Ministry will have to be built—a ministry structure into which the people with pastoral gifts can flow. This will mean that the right people will be in the right places for the right reasons doing the right things.

"He who has an ear, let him hear what the Spirit says to the church-es." Enable your people to know what their spiritual gifts are and what to do with them.

Notes

1. Robert E. Slocum, *Maximize Your Ministry* (Colorado Springs: Navpress, 1990), pp. 170, 257.
2. Ibid., p. 9.
3. Ibid., p. 170.
4. Ibid., p. 257.
5. The Greek word for *man* is *anthropos*, meaning a human being, whether male or female; referring to the genus or nature, not to gender. *We* at the beginning of verse 6 clarifies the inclusiveness of *man*. It does not distinguish between man and woman, but between humans and animals, between human beings and God.
6. Ibid., Slocum develops this position on pages 74 and 166-198.
7. "Leadership," *Christianity Today* (fall 1996): 62.

An Egalitarian Church

CLASSLESS AND "MINISTRY-BLIND"

Suppose I am a layperson, sitting in my pew on a Sunday morning. While listening to the preacher, the following questions and thoughts are chasing each other around in my head:

1. *Why am I here and he there? Is he better than I? Is he more important than I? Do I rank lower than he?*

There is no question that...

- *He is good; his sermons are inspiring, interesting and informative.*
- *He is important; he is preaching the Word of God, and that is important.*
- *He ranks high; he is credentialed, respected and called to be the spiritual leader of the congregation. That's why he's there and I am here.*

2. *He is a man of God. His prayers get through to God. He knows his Bible. He gives himself to serve God. That pulpit really sets him apart as "a man of God."*

chapter three

There is no question that...

- *He is a man of God; he is a servant of God, loves God and seems very close to God.*
- *He has the ability to pray; he can find the right words and express them in earnest.*
- *He deserves to be in the pulpit; God called him into the ministry. He is a minister. That's why he's there and I am here.*

3. *If I want to truly serve God, be important in the Church, rank high among Christians and do significant ministry, I will have to change my course in life, go to seminary and be ordained. A long pause to ruminate. There must be a serious error in my thinking. I'll have to ponder this later, because I truly want to serve God.*

Later ponderings expose that the error is mine, thinking that...

- *Because he is good at preaching, important to the church and ranks high as spiritual leader of the congregation; and because I am not qualified to preach, am not as prominent in the church and not the spiritual leader of the congregation, I am a second-class Christian.*
- *Because I am not an ordained minister, I am not called by God.*
- *Because he is ordained, he is better than I.*
- *Because he is there and I am here, I rank lower than he.*
- *Because he is behind the pulpit, he is a minister and I am something less.*
- *His closeness to God, his passion for ministry and his advanced spirituality is only for special people such as he whom God calls into the ordained ministry.*

Still more ponderings and later discoveries from discussion and Scripture reveal the deeper truth that...

1. *I also am called to do ministry. My call to ministry was given along with my call to faith. It's part of the new birth, included in my baptism.*

2. *I also have been given spiritual gifts for ministry. Because it is the Spirit of God who gives the gifts, every ministry is significant and every volunteer and vocational minister is important to the Church.*

3. *I also am a minister. The difference between my ministry and his is function, not order. He is a specialist in his; I am a specialist in mine. Together we get God's work done.*

4. *I also have full access to the power of God for effective ministry.*

5. *I also need to be equipped, not for preaching, but for what God called me to do—not by going to seminary, but by taking advantage of training opportunities in my church and community.*

6. *I also have authority to do my ministry. His authority and my authority both come from God, not from credentials.*

The office of pastor is considered by most people to be the highest position in the Church. This notion, however common, is an unfortunate development because it has forged a dichotomy, creating two classes of Christians: laity and clergy.

The origin of this error is traced to the fourth century when the Church adopted the hierarchical structure of the Roman empire, instead of staying with the New Testament "body" model. This historical development demonstrates how secular culture bonds with Christian culture. This bonding is sometimes a blessing and sometimes a curse. In this case it has been a curse because the hierarchical model replaced the "body" model. Paul's description of how the Church works as a body has been all but lost through the centuries:

> Those parts of the body that seem to be weaker are indispensable, and the parts that we think are less honorable we treat with special honor....God has combined the members of the body and has given greater honor to the parts that lacked it, so that there should be no division in the body, but that its parts should have equal concern for each other (1 Cor. 12:22-25).

Many churches are breaking free from this historical bond replacing the multi-level hierarchical way of being God's people to the every-member-equal "body" way of being God's people.

chapter three

Today's traditional church, however, perpetuates this two-class order. This distortion erroneously continues to mislead Christians into believing that if they want to *really* serve God, they must leave their communities, go to seminary, be ordained and become pastors of local churches.

Not until the 1950s did the Church begin to awaken to a better way of doing God's business. It rediscovered the biblical model for ministry. Ephesians 4:11,12 sharply focuses it by enjoining pastors and teachers to equip the saints for the work of ministry. The context and other Scriptures make it unmistakably clear that every Christian is a minister. So many churches of all denominations are participating in this rediscovery that the result is nothing less than a second Reformation.

In the first Reformation, the Church gave the Bible to the people. In the second Reformation, the Church is giving the ministry to the people. The Church is again becoming a classless Church. The disparity of laity and clergy is being replaced by the parity of all the people of God (the *laos*).

How did the Church we inherited arrive at this separation between clergy and laity and hierarchy? We need to know, for retracing our steps will help us to correct our course. The answer starts in the Old Testament and follows five trail markers to the present.

Marker 1: A Special Order of Priests
In Old Testament Israel the priestly order separated priests from the rest of the people. They led the rituals, represented the people to God and received provision for their material needs from the people. Israelites who were not from the tribe of Levi could not join this order.

Marker 2: All Are Priests
The New Testament does not provide evidence of an order of priests. Jesus' coming ended that order (see Heb. 4—5). The Church of Jesus Christ *in toto* is a "royal priesthood" (1 Pet. 2:9). All Christians are given gifts for ministry. There is only one order: *laos*, "the people of God." All are ministers. All are priests. All are "called." Oscar Feucht, a Missouri Synod Lutheran Church theologian and churchman, wrote in his significantly titled book, *Everyone A Minister*:

> The Old Testament distinction between priest and people, clergymen and laymen, is at an end. Christ, our High

Priest, has made all Christians priests before God. All Christians are God's clergy, and there is no special clerical order in the Church.[1]

Church historian Kenneth Scott Latourette writes about how strongly Martin Luther believed in the equality of Christians:

> Luther maintained that the works of priests and members of the religious orders are not a whit more sacred in the sight of God than those of a farmer in his fields or of a woman in her household duties.[2]

Marker 3: One Order, Many Functions

The differences between laity and clergy are not in *order*, but in *function*. Peter's definition of the Church—a "royal priesthood"—establishes the fact that only one order exists. That one order is priest (or minister), however, God has given it many functions. The function we are exploring in this book is pastoral care. *Pastor*, therefore, is understood to be a function, not an order.

In, *Why Priests? A Proposal for a New Church Ministry*, Hans Küng concludes that the New Testament does not really speak of a fixed church office. It uses a variety of terms almost interchangeably. The clergy office is not institutionalized.[3]

Marker 4: A New Order, Clergy

The unfortunate two-order change began with one of the greatest events in Church history, the Edict of Constantine in A.D. 312. Until that time the Church had been persecuted by Roman emperors. But during a dream on October 28, A.D. 312, Emperor Constantine saw a cross in the sky accompanied with the words "In this sign conquer." Thus, he conquered; then looked upon his brilliant military victory as proof of Christ's power and the superiority of the Christian religion. He legalized Christianity. The Church was suddenly favored and pampered.

The Church began to adopt the hierarchical structure of the Roman government, thereby starting its drift from the New Testament "body" design. The hierarchical structure elevated some functions and people over others, creating descending degrees of importance.

This caste system was antithetical to Christ's teaching, which opposed vying to be greatest in His kingdom (see Mark 10:35-45).

The division between clergy and laity took shape. The clergy preached, taught, pastored and created forms of worship. The people were expected to pray and pay. (One contemporary interprets it: "Lay people are asked to show up, pay up and shut up.") By the twelfth century, the canon lawyer Gratian wrote in his decretals: "There are two kinds of Christians, the clergy who are to be devoted to the divine office...and the other sort of Christians who are called 'lay folk.'"[4]

The Church formed special orders from what were originally functions. For example, the pastors and teachers from the list of five ministries in Ephesians 4:11 are not classical orders in the Church, but are the functions of those to whom Christ gave pastoral and teaching gifts. The Church drifted into the error of institutionalizing these functions, making orders of them, elevating the people in these orders to levels of greater importance.

Marker 5: Rediscovery of the Priesthood of Believers

At times the Church struggled to free itself from the vise grip of hierarchy. The sixteenth century Reformation led by Martin Luther not only rediscovered *justification by faith*, but also rediscovered the *priesthood of believers*. *Priesthood* includes two roles: (1) *priest*, representing people to God; and (2) *minister*, doing service for God.

The Reformation regarded every believer to be a priest and every believer to be a minister. The Church continued to follow the "every believer a priest" reform, but because the grip of the two-class system was so powerful, the "every believer is a minister" reform failed. Not until the 1950s did the Church rekindle its struggle for this reform. Since then, multitudes of church leaders and congregations have broken free by rediscovering what had been lost from the New Testament model wherein every Christian is a minister, and that the differentiation between Christians is *function*—not *order*.

The awakened Church today is winning the struggle. It is releasing the power of the laity by giving ministry back to them, and releasing a new power in the clergy by restoring the clergy's function of equipping the laity to do the ministry. The historic meaning of the New Testament Greek word, *laos*, is again beginning to resound: "the people of God."

The Church can once again be classless, including both clergy and laity in one order—*laos*. As *laos*, clergy are now fulfilling their divinely-ordered roles, as *ministers*, not as *The Ministers*, whose function it is to equip other Christians for their ministries. As *laos*, laypeople are now fulfilling their divinely-ordered roles, doing the ministries for which they have been gifted. The second Reformation regards every Christian as a first-class Christian.

Jesus preeminently models all of the foregoing principles for an egalitarian church in the one act of washing His disciples' feet. If one picture is worth a thousand words, the following scene is worth a million:

> After that, he poured water into a basin and began to wash his disciples' feet, drying them with the towel that was wrapped around him....When he had finished washing their feet, he put on his clothes and returned to his place. "Do you understand what I have done for you?" he asked them...."I have set you an example that you should do as I have done for you....Now that you know these things, you will be blessed if you do them" (John 13:5,12,15,17).

Let's examine how He models these principles.

HE WAS A SERVANT

He washed His disciples' feet. He was a servant doing a servant's task. His serving unveiled a hard-to-see part of His nature. The Gospels tell mostly of His power, knowledge and wisdom. This one servile act, however, gives a kaleidoscopic twist to all of His acts, revealing Him as a servant.

He served His Father by doing His Father's will; He served the sick by healing them; He served the 5,000 by feeding them. Long before washing His disciples' feet, Jesus made it clear that He came into the world not to be served, but to serve (see Matt. 20:28). He had a true "servant spirit."

What in *our* spirits causes us clergy to use our education, ordination and prominence for self-aggrandizement, distorting our understanding of greatness and deceiving us into thinking that menial tasks are beneath our positions? Laypeople participate in this massive error by believing clergy live on this artificially elevated level. Jesus' example exposes this error.

We have His Spirit (see Rom. 8:9) and His mind (1 Cor. 2:16). Let's use them!

HE EXCELLED IN SERVING

He excelled in all qualities: teaching, prayer, healing and now serving. And He excelled without an air of superiority. The Lord, on His knees before His disciples, basin and towel in hand, revealed the full spectrum of greatness. He was true Lord and true servant.

I am reminded of two clergy friends who exhibit excellence in serving. They regularly help clear the tables after church dinners, taking the plates and silver to the kitchen. One always arrives early to help set up the room or prepare and serve the meals. They feel as much at home while serving in the dining room week-day nights as they do serving in the sanctuary Sunday mornings. This is not put on; it is their nature.

HE WAS EGALITARIAN (CLASSLESS)

Even though He was their rabbi and Lord, He thought of His disciples as brothers and friends (see Matt. 12:49; John 15:15). He did not flaunt His position, privately or publicly, inwardly or outwardly, subconsciously or consciously.

He accepted His role of great responsibility (forming the foundation for their faith and lives) and high prominence (rabbi, Son of God and healer) without creating a disparity that would have put Him in one class and them in another. He made it clear that He was merely fulfilling His Father's will. Their parity lay in the fact that they, too, were to fulfill their Father's will.

HE AFFIRMED DIFFERENCES WITHOUT DISPARITY

He said, "You call me 'Teacher' and 'Lord,' and rightfully so, for that is what I am" (John 13:13). The disciples were His pupils. However, this difference implied neither a greater/lesser nor higher/lower level of importance.

Peter, because he could think only in the categories of greater/lesser and higher/lower, was not about to permit Jesus to be his servant. It must be that he did not yet truly know Jesus, for he denied Him His desire to serve: "No...you shall never wash my feet" (v. 8). To Peter, washing feet was beneath Jesus' dignity. To Jesus, it was an integral part of what He came into the world to do. He had served by teaching, healing, feeding, comforting and setting the record straight with the religious leaders. He was now serving by washing feet. A few hours later, He would perform the ultimate service, giving His life for His friends.

We in the Church need to take His counsel, "I have set you an example that you should do as I have done for you" (v. 15).

I derived two essentials from Jesus' example for my own growth in this area, which I hope to pass on to you individually and to the Church at large.

First, Jesus demonstrated that differences do exist among Christians in their church lives; but the differences are in *function*, not in *order*. By order, I mean rank, class, status, breed, genre, grade, caste, type or species. There is one order in the Church—*laos*, the people of God. Jesus affirmed one order when He declared, "Whoever does God's will is my brother and sister" (Mark 3:35).

Differences also exist in function, however, they are *utilitarian*. They do not infer differences in rank, worth or importance of a person, but differences in kinds of service. Jesus taught that our common denominator is doing the Father's will.

Second, Jesus needed to extricate Himself from Peter's mental prison. As long as Peter considered Jesus above washing feet, Jesus could not serve Peter without forcing Himself on him. The mental prisons in which people lock their pastors and in which pastors lock their people confine them to these roles.

When I was a pastor in Hawaii, I experienced imprisonment in the minds of the people. They loved me. (The spirit of aloha is real.) I was their *kahu* (the Hawaiian word for "shepherd"). However, these people held me in such high regard that it seemed I was in a different world. Because of this, I was unable to be a "friend" and "brother" to them. Part of me loved it. They pampered me. They were awestruck in my presence. I was untouchable. Little children looked up at me as though I were deity.

Another part of me resisted this lofty position because it was not my true self. The *kahu* mold they had pressed me into prevented most of them from getting to know me; and I didn't get to know them either. I felt that my ministry among them was seriously limited because it seemed impossible to disengage myself from the role in which they had cast me.

> When people put us on a pedestal, the temptation is not only to enjoy it, but also to take advantage of it.

Jesus was not about to let Peter imprison Him in a superior upper-level role. He freed Himself by harsh words to Peter. Peter acquiesced, and was then able to grasp a more complete picture of who Jesus was: servant first and foremost.

Clergy need to extricate themselves both from the role in which the traditional church has cast them, and the role in which they have traditionally cast themselves. Laity need to extricate themselves from the role in which the traditional church has cast them and from the role in which the traditional pastor casts them. If they are not both set free from their tradition-set roles, their respective ministries will be seriously hampered.

HE IS OUR EXAMPLE

Five of Jesus' words say it all: "Do as I have done." If we are not serving, we imply that we are better than our Lord. This is arrogance! If we accept and perpetuate the traditional two-order dichotomy, we imply that we are above our Lord. This is disdain! He neutralized two-level thinking every time it raised its ugly head; He "nipped it in the bud."

There are two examples of this. First, as we have seen, Peter forbade Jesus to wash His feet. But Jesus repudiated him, telling Peter that if he wanted to be part of His life, he would accept the washing. Peter accepted. When people put us on a pedestal, the temptation is not only to enjoy it, but also to take advantage of it. If Jesus had responded like many in the traditional church, He would have had Peter washing *His* feet.

Second, James and John vied with the other 10 disciples for the highest position in Christ's kingdom (see Mark 10:35-38). The others were indignant. Their request rankled the others and threatened to divide them into two camps. Jesus put an end to this brazen lust for privilege by telling the Twelve they didn't know what they were asking for. The two-storied traditional church needs the same rebuke.

If we continue to tolerate the two-class distinction in the Church without taking action to challenge and change it, we have sided with the element Jesus put down; we disregard the example He set for His Church. Shall we call our disregard, rebellion, pride, nose-thumbing and arrogance disobedience or sin? We need to hear Jesus: "Now that you know these things, you will be blessed if you do them" (John 13:17).

We might call a one-class, one-level, egalitarian church a *ministry-blind* church. The term piggybacks "color-blind," a term describing a person who does not "see" differences in the color of people's skin. The *ministry-blind* church neither treats one ministry as more important than another, nor one minister as higher than another. *Ministry-blindness* enables us to see the variety of Christians performing their variety of functions all as *laos*, the people of God.

In the traditional church,[5] one ministry is seen as more important than another and one minister as higher than another. I believe the Presbyterian Church (USA) is trying to do something about this by no longer using the designation *Senior Pastor* in the Book of Order, replacing it with *Pastor, Head of Staff*. This is an attempt, small as it may be, to focus on function rather than office.

The Corinthian Christians wrongly perceived differences between their leaders. Some believed Paul was better than Apollos. Others were sure Apollos was better than Paul. Some felt that Cephas was the greatest. Not to be outdone by any of the preceding, some arrogantly claimed to follow Christ.

They quarreled. They divided into camps, lining up behind their champions: "I follow Paul"; another, "I follow Apollos"; another, "I follow Cephas"; still another, "I follow Christ" (1 Cor. 1:12). Paul appealed to them to be "perfectly united in mind and thought" (v. 10).

Christ was not divided, he wrote. Paul was not crucified for them. Paul pressed them to see that there was no difference in order, that there was no difference in importance, that their ministries complemented rather than competed with each other.

"What, after all, is Apollos? And what is Paul? Only servants, through whom you came to believe—as the Lord has assigned to each his task. I planted the seed, Apollos watered it, but God made it grow" (3:5,6).

Unity was of supreme importance to Paul, therefore he carried this issue forward: "So neither he who plants nor he who waters is anything, but only God, who makes things grow" (3:7). Planter and waterer are one in purpose. Both are faithful servants of God. Neither could boast in *what* they did, for this was determined by God. The tribute was to God who called them and who made their service effective, not to themselves. End of subject? Not quite.

Lest their false perceptions of different ratings between their leaders metastasize to their perceptions of differences among themselves, Paul hastens to explain that they are God's temples. The Spirit of God is in each of them. Then he moves on with these words:

> So then, no more boasting about men! All things are yours, whether Paul or Apollos or Cephas or the world or life or death or the present or the future—all are yours, and you are of Christ, and Christ is of God. So then, men ought to regard us as servants of Christ (1 Cor. 3:21—4:1).

When Paul was on one of his missionary journeys, he had to disclaim superiority attributed to him by pagans who regarded him as the god, Hermes. He now had to disclaim superiority to the Christians who regarded him as towering above them. In pagan Lystra, Paul shouted to the crowd wanting to offer sacrifices to him. "Why are you doing this? We too are only men, human like you. We are bringing you good news" (Acts 14:15). Now in the Church he rebuked the Christians, declaring that he was no more than a servant, obligated to do what God assigned him.

The apostle Paul modeled egalitarianism.

He was a *father* without being paternalistic.
He was an *apostle* without being dictatorial.
He was a *leader* without being domineering.
He was an *authority* without being authoritarian.
He was an *example* without being proud.
He was an *equal* without abdicating his authority.
He *corrected* without controlling.
He *taught* without demagoguery.
He *advised* without being officious.
He *persuaded* without manipulation.
He *exhorted* without vindictiveness.
He *compromised* without sacrificing his convictions.
He *suffered* without self-pity.
He *adapted* without losing integrity.
He saw himself a *servant*; we see him a master.
He saw himself a *sinner*; we see him a saint.
He saw himself the *least apostle*; we see him the greatest.[6]

How far the Church has moved from the egalitarian character of the man who had a greater impact on the Church than any other human! How sad that the Church drifted into its split-level, hierarchical aberration centuries ago and continues to perpetuate this malformation! What a need for contemporary leaders to shout to the crowd, "We are

> Functions unite rather than separate;
> they complement rather than compete,
> just like the many members of a
> healthy human body.

only human like you!" Praise God, increasing numbers of leaders *are* shouting in our day. The volume is increasing. Every church leader and every church member should help raise the volume.

Only in a one-level, classless church can all members be recognized as fully accredited ministers. Only there are members as free to do *their* ministries as vocational ministers are, the ministries for which

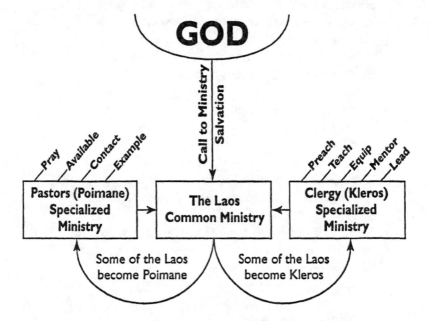

God gave them the necessary gifts and to which He is calling them. The diagram⁷ above helps to understand the egalitarian dynamic.

The diagram could be extended to include many additional curved arrows flowing from the "common ministry" pool to other specialized ministries such as evangelism, social issues, cross-cultural ministry, community improvement organizations, youth ministry and on and on.

Notice that clergy are not put down and laity are not raised up. Instead, we are all joined together at the highest level for redeemed folks, *laos*, the people of God. No clergy bashing occurs (of which I have been accused at times); and no need for anti-clericalism (which has taken place at times throughout Church history). We are one in Christ and one in ministry. Only our functions differ. And functions unite rather than separate; they complement rather than compete, just like the many members of a healthy human body.

But what about obvious differences? Isn't there an obvious distinction between the pastor of a church and an usher? Yes, and no. In the church we can affirm differentiation in function without creating differences in rank. Our problem is that we see the church as an organization like any other organization in our community. The CEO is on top—greater responsibility, more power and enviable prestige—while one of the auditors is at the bottom.

Our culture reinforces hierarchical thinking. We erroneously equate the pastor of a church with the CEO, and one of the ushers with the auditor. We rank one higher than the other, thereby unavoidably ranking the other lower. Because this is the way it is done in the kingdom of our world, we think it must be the way to do it in the kingdom of God. Not so!

The disturbing fact about Jesus' teaching on greatness and the example He set is that if we believe what He taught and if we follow His example, we are at odds with our culture. We are in a bind, because if we don't believe and follow Him, we are at odds with Him. He taught:

> You know that those who are regarded as rulers of the Gentiles lord it over them, and their high officials exercise authority over them. *Not so with you* (italics mine). Instead, whoever wants to become great among you must be your servant, and whoever wants to be first must be slave of all (Mark 10:42-45).

A church may have a slick, enviable organization by adopting the business model, but that is about all it will be—a slick, enviable organization. The biblical model is that of a body, where each part, though different from all the others, is equally important and exists to serve all the other parts.

Differences in the Church are not to be compared with the difference between the CEO and an auditor, but with the difference between the head and the feet of a body, each indispensable to the whole. My paraphrase of 1 Corinthians 12:22-25 (quoted previously in this chapter), which I believe catches the true meaning for how the church is to function today, reads as follows:

> Those Christians who are serving in ways which do not seem as important as others are indispensable, and the functions we think are less honorable we treat with special honor. God has combined the members of the church into one body and has given greater honor to those who

lacked it, so there should be no division between lay and clergy. All parts of the body should accept all the other parts as equals.

The differences, then, are utilitarian. They are functional differences, assigned by our Lord so all of His work can be carried on:

All these [differences in faith, prophecy, etc.] are the work of one and the same Spirit, and he gives them to each one, just as he determines [or "just as he assigns"] (1 Cor. 12:11).

But to each one of us grace [for ministering] has been given as Christ apportioned it [or "as Christ assigned it"] (Eph. 4:7).

Each one should use whatever gift he has received [or "has been assigned"] to serve others (1 Pet. 4:10).

Each one of us is dependent upon all the others for doing our part. "A chain is only as strong as its weakest link." Any one person can curb the effectiveness of a whole group. Likewise, any one person can augment the effectiveness of the whole group.

Two equalizing agents are prevalent in the Church: interdependence and mission. No one person can function effectively in the mission Christ committed to that individual independent from others. Think of the disaster of The Challenger, the space rocket that exploded seconds after liftoff, killing all seven astronauts. What was the relative importance of the person who designed the O ring and the commander? Interdependence and mission put them on the same level, regardless of titles, rank and name plates.

So, each person is an equally significant participant in the mission of the Church and equally dependent upon the others.

Because the Scriptures recognize only one order in the Church, the differences among us can be only in the diversity of functions God assigned to that one order. Then there are recognizable differences within each function:

Utilitarian Differences
We differ, but our differences are in what we do, not in who we are. The Church is an organism, not an organization; but even organisms

have to be organized. Someone has to be president, moderator, director, coordinator, etc.

Quality Differences
Variety of experience, training, abilities and skills: careful/careless, thorough/incomplete, effective/ineffective.

Personality Differences
Introvert/extrovert, warm/formal, loquacious/laconic, activistic/quietistic.

Maturity Differences
New Christian/seasoned Christian, wise/not-so-wise, well-read/not-so-well-read, milk/solid food (see 1 Cor. 3:2).

Training Differences
High school/college, workshops/seminary, life experiences/formal education.

Effectiveness Differences
Persuasive/weak, impressive/unimpressive.

Commitment Differences
Total/partial, Christ-centered/self-centered, spiritual/worldly.

Age Differences
14/84, 25/50, Generation X/senior.

Other legitimate differences also exist. Paul recognized them. He wrote to his friends in Philippi that he had no one like Timothy to send to them (see Phil. 2:20,21). Everyone else looked out for their own interests, not the interest of others. When it came to this man's passion for others-centered ministry, he was head and shoulders above the rest.

Epaphroditus was also singled out for commendation: "honor men like him" (Phil. 2:29,30). His surpassing passion for ministry put him at physical risk. He almost died for the work of Christ.

So within the ministry, inequality of excellence exists, not because of the nature of us humans, but because of the nature of commitment.

And this can be nonjudgmentally recognized: "honor to whom honor [is due]" (Rom. 13:7, *NASB*).

Paul wrote that elders who direct the affairs of the church *well* are worthy of double honor. Can we assume that some did not do as well as others? Certainly. There will always be a difference in quality and effectiveness. But these performance variations do not challenge the fact that there is no difference in order.

I believe Jesus referred to performance differences in His parable of the talents (see Matt. 25:14-30). Even though each of the two who performed increased his money 100 percent, the actual number of dollars differed. The one with five thousand dollars gained five thousand more; the one with two thousand gained two thousand more. The difference made no difference to the master for he equally commended both. It was the one who did nothing with his talent who was in trouble.

Recognizing differences in excellence should challenge every one of us to maximize our ministry, to strive to reach our highest potential. Watching brothers and sisters whose spirits are bursting with enthusiasm for ministry and who excel in performance should prod others of us to dedicate our giftedness to perfection and to deny halfheartedness and mediocrity. Could Peter have been referring to excellence in ministry when he used the word *faithfully* in his counsel to Christians: "Each one...*faithfully* administering God's grace [or ministry] in its various forms" (1 Pet. 4:10)?

All are first-class Christians, but all may not be doing a first-class job. All are in the one order, *laos*, but all may not be doing ministry as well as they could be doing it. The idea is not to compare ourselves with others to see if we are doing ministry as well as they, for that would lead to gross wrong; but to compare how we are doing ministry with how we *could* be doing it.

This is the sense of Hebrews 10:24: "Let us consider how we may spur one another on toward love and good deeds." Observing people who are doing ministry well should spur us on, not to do it as well as they, but to do it the very best *we* are capable of doing it. We actually may be capable of doing it better than they if we apply the same energy and spirit.

By reading this far, you now possess a body of truth, a newly recovered cache, about how Christ is building His Church in our era: egal-

itarian, classless, "ministry-blind," one order. What can you do with
it? Because truth is power, and because truth is for a purpose, the following are some tailored uses for this truth:

> **For leaders:** This truth arms you with the rationale to lib-
> erate your church from the confines of traditionalism and
> to lead it onward into new frontiers of lay ministry. This is
> a fair application of Jesus' confidence in the power of
> truth: "You shall know the truth and the truth shall make
> you free" (John 8:32, *NASB*). Preach it, teach it, love it, talk
> about it, create structures to house it. *Let laypeople do it!*

> **For church members:** This truth assures you of your parity
> with the clergy. It authorizes you to stand before a mirror
> (as one layperson told me she did) watching yourself artic-
> ulate, "I am a minister!" Visualize both you and the clergy
> as *laos,* the people of God. Believe it, talk it up, pray about
> what you should do. Then take action. *Let laypeople do it!*

> **For your church:** If your church's culture does not include
> "every member is a minister," work together to change the
> culture. Culture change can start with preaching, but
> preaching alone will not do it. Culture change is far more
> than starting a new program. Culture change is a paradigm
> shift from the traditional model to the new. It requires a
> change of what you believe, how you see yourself, how
> you see one another and what you do. *Let laypeople do it!*

> **For the Church at large:** Paul Stevens said it best:
> "Without every-member-ministry, we have unlived bibli-
> cal truths, unstrategic leadership deployment, untapped
> resources in the congregation and an unreached world!"[8]
> *Let laypeople do it!*

If you are going to do something with this truth, you have to begin
somewhere. Start with giving the pastoral care of the congregation to
laypeople. The format for doing this is provided in appendix H of this
book. Hundreds of churches are using our Lay Pastors Ministry

model and discovering that laypeople are also gifted for ministry, are also called by God to do ministry and are as turned on by doing pastoral care as vocational pastors. "He who has an ear, let him hear what the Spirit says to the churches." *Let laypeople do it!*

Notes:

1. Oscar E. Feucht, *Everyone A Minister* (St. Louis: Concordia Publishing House, 1994), p. 64.

2. Kenneth Scott Latourette, *A History of Christianity, Volume II*, as quoted by George G. Hunter III in his book *Church for the Unchurched*, p. 121.

3. Patricia Page, *All God's People Are Ministers*, (Minneapolis: Augsburg Fortress, 1993), pp. 36-37.

4. Ibid., p. 64.

5. When I use the phrase "the traditional Church," I am referring to the Church universal from A.D. 312 to the 1950s, the Christendom period as defined by Loren Mead in his book, *The Once and Future Church* (Washington, D.C.: The Alban Institute, 1991) pp. 13-22. He describes it as hierarchical, over-institutionalized and divided into two classes of Christians: clergy and laity. Many churches are traditional, trying to do business as usual and will barely limp into the next century without changing. Their cry is, "If only things could be the way they were!" while we say, "If only things were the way they could be!"

6. These biblical references, line by line, are for those who wish to study this part of Paul's life and ministry: father (1 Cor. 4:15; 1 Tim. 1:2); apostle (Rom. 1:1; 1 Cor. 15:9,10); leader (Acts 20:13-38); authority (1 Cor. 11:17-34); example (1 Cor. 4:16; 1 Thess. 1:6); equal (1 Cor. 5:18-21; Phil. 4:3; 1 Thess. 3:2; Philem. 24); corrected (1 Cor. 5:1-5; Phil. 4:2); advised (1 Tim. 2:1-6; 2 Tim 2:14-19); persuaded (Acts 17:16-34); exhorted (1 Tim. 1:3-7); compromised (Acts 16:3); suffered (Phil. 1:12-14; 4:10-13); adapted (1 Cor. 9:22); servant (Rom. 1:1; 1 Cor. 3:5; 4:1); sinner (Rom. 7:14-24; 1 Tim. 1:15,16); least apostle (1 Cor. 15:9).

7. For the basic idea of this diagram, I am indebted to James L. Garlow for his book, *Partners in Ministry* (Kansas City, Mo.: Beacon Hill Press, 1982) p. 43.

8. R. Paul Stevens and Phil Collins, *The Equipping Pastor* (Washington, D.C.: The Alban Institute, 1993) p. XI.

A Ministry-Balanced Church

THE GREAT COMMISSION: THE GREAT CHARTER

The headwaters of the Mississippi River in Minnesota's Itasca State Park have been the starting point of long canoe trips for many adventurers. My family and I camped at this beautiful site years ago. I recall how thrilled we were to step from rock to rock over the narrow beginnings of one of the two greatest rivers in the western hemisphere. After leaving Lake Itasca, the mighty Mississippi wends its way 2,000 miles to the Gulf of Mexico.

The other great river—the Amazon—is in South America. These two prominent streams have something in common: they become part of a far greater body of water, the Atlantic Ocean.

Two great streams of another nature flow through the New Testament, joining their waters in the greater ocean of God's love. One stream is the Great Commission, the mandate of our Lord to go make disciples of all nations (see Matt. 28:19,20). The other may not sound as familiar. It is the Great Charter, the mandate of our Lord to take care of His sheep (see John 21:16). The one calls for the Church to make disciples; the other, to care for those disciples.

The church in which the Lay Pastors Ministry can happen will strive to equalize these two streams. On the one hand, they will deploy those gifted and called to make disciples in ministries designed for missions and evangelism. On the other hand, they will deploy those gifted and called to care for Christ's followers in ministries designed for pastoral care. Neither is done at the neglect of the other: not "either-or," but "both-and." Balance is the key.

I believe God raised up the Lay Pastors Ministry to help fulfill the Great Charter. There is no thought of disparaging the Great Commission (much of my own ministry energy throughout the years has been invested in making disciples), but because Scripture places such a heavy emphasis on lay pastoral care, my emphasis is on the one stream I call the Great Charter.

History records the Magna Carta—meaning the Great Charter—as a constitution guaranteeing fundamental personal and other rights, wrested from King John by the English barons on June 15, 1215. I call 1 Peter 5:1-4 the Magna Carta of the Lay Pastors Ministry because this model of congregational care guarantees the fundamental personal right of every church member to pastoral care:

> To the elders among you, I appeal as a fellow elder, a witness of Christ's sufferings and one who also will share in the glory to be revealed: Be shepherds of God's flock that is under your care, serving as overseers—not because you must, but because you are willing, as God wants you to be; not greedy for money, but eager to serve; not lording it over those entrusted to you, but being examples to the flock. And when the Chief Shepherd appears, you will receive the crown of glory that will never fade away.

The flow of the Great Commission through the New Testament is well known. To its credit, the Church has plied these waters with great success for the past three centuries. the Great Charter is not well known. I invite you to accompany me through the New Testament for the grand experience of exploring these less familiar waters.

We begin at the headwaters. Three bubbling springs feed this great flow of pastoral care:

- Jesus' mandate: "A new commandment I give you [My disciples]: Love *one another*" (John 13:34).

- Jesus' prayer: "I pray for *them* [My disciples]. I am *not* praying for the world, but for *those you have given me*" (17:9).
- Jesus' charge: "Take care of *my sheep*" (21:16).

The italics, of course, are mine. They make it obvious that Jesus places great importance on caring for those who are already His. A misinterpretation of this selective attention risks Christian elitism. It comes dangerously close to claiming that only Christians matter to God.

This thinking, of course, is ridiculous. After all, Jesus' earlier call to Peter to make disciples—"Follow me and I will make you [a fisher] of men" (Matt. 4:19)—predates this call to take care of His sheep. He struck a balance between the two ministries.

The elitist risk wakes us up! It opens our eyes to the fact that when people come to Christ and join our churches, they have a right to be loved, heard, nurtured, prayed for and encouraged. They have a right to pastoral care. The Great Charter guarantees this right.

We now journey downstream to Acts. The caring dynamic was given a practical spin when the apostles chose seven people to take responsibility—not for all people in the community, but for the widows in their church (see Acts 6:1-7). Moving on, we hear Paul instructing the elders of the Ephesian church: "Keep watch over yourselves and all the flock of which the Holy Spirit has made you overseers. Be shepherds of the church of God" (20:28). He made no reference to making more disciples.

Next, we sail through Romans. Again, as though the world did not matter, the Church is seen as a Body that includes only Christians—"each member belongs to all the others" (Rom. 12:5). It is a closed fellowship. The seven gifts listed in Romans 12:4-8 are all intended to be used within the Body. This is followed by, "Be devoted *to one another* in brotherly love" (v. 10, italics mine) Sounds exclusive, doesn't it?

On down the river—the 14 spiritual gifts listed in 1 Corinthians 12 are for those who confess, "Jesus is Lord" (v. 3), and are to be used within the Church. In Galatians 6, the apostle asks for the preferential treatment of believers, "Let us do good to all people, *especially to those who belong to the family of believers*" (v. 10, italics mine).

The waters widen in Ephesians 4, calling pastors and teachers to prepare God's people for works of service. For what purpose? Evangelism? Missions? Making disciples? Not at this time The purpose is to build up the Body of Christ, promote unity and further the maturity of the saints.

Like the Mississippi River at Lake Pipen on the Minnesota-Wisconsin border, the stream through the New Testament widens at 1 Peter 5:1-4. Peter, who was called by Jesus first to fish for people and later to take care of His sheep, appeals to the elders of five Roman provinces to do what? Make disciples? Not at this time. His appeal is that they shepherd God's flock. Have we explored this stream sufficiently to make the point?

If a person were to read only the parts of the New Testament calling Christians to love one another, to tend the flock, to shepherd God's people and to give preferential treatment to Christians, he or she would think that the Church's energies are to be consumed only on itself at the exclusion of those outside the Church. It would appear that *the Great Charter* is the only mission of the Church.

Conversely, if a person were to read only the parts of the New Testament calling Christians to make disciples of all nations, to evangelize and seek the lost (as in Jesus' parable of the one lost sheep in Luke 15), he or she would believe that the Church's energies are to be consumed only on those outside of the fold. It would appear that *the Great Commission* is the only mission of the Church.

To avoid this "either/or" absurdity, we must accept the whole counsel of God and believe that both are absolute imperatives for Christ's Church. Every Christian is to be committed to both. However, no one can be productively engaged in both at the same time. It is not humanly possible for any one person to give himself or herself concurrently to both of these demanding, all-consuming ministries.

God knows this, therefore, He gives a variety of gifts and calls, each Christian to a chosen ministry. The idea is: support both; do one. Paraphrasing Romans 12:6-8 illumines this:

> If a man's gift is *making disciples*, let him use it in proportion to his faith; if it is *pastoring*, let him care for God's people diligently.

God gives gifts for one stream to some people, and gifts for the other stream to other people. His plan for keeping a balance between the two and getting both done is to mobilize the *laos*—all the people of God—to assist them in discovering their ministries, to equip them, to commission them and to release them to do what God has called them to do. It takes all the people of God to do all the work of God.

The idea of the Great Charter is new to many churches. For example, my vacation travels took me through a city in which a church famous for its evangelism program was located. On the spur of the moment I stopped in, hoping to meet the minister of pastoral care. It was his day off, but I was able to visit with his secretary. As I inquired about their program for pastoral care, hoping to pick up some ideas for

> Pastoring follows evangelism in the spiritual order just as nurturing follows birth in the biological order.

my own ministry, she became tearful. She began to pour her heart out as she told me a story she had needed to tell somebody for a long time.

In order to pastorally care for the hundreds of people who were joining the church as the result of their effective evangelism program, only one person was ministering. It was her boss, and he was burning out. Consequently, people were not only joining the church, but they were also leaving it.

The church was remarkably successful in evangelism, recruiting hundreds of people to visit in homes, share the gospel and assist people in making their decision to receive Christ and join the church. Without question God had given hundreds of other members of the church pastoral gifts, but because the Great Commission dominated, the Great Charter didn't have a chance. The result was that the back door of the church, as they say, was nearly as busy as the front door. The two mighty ministries of the church were woefully out of balance.

The apostle Paul brought these two into balance in his ministry. But in the Church as I know it, we don't hear about his pastoral work. His fame as an evangelist and church planter overshadows what I call his "second ministry." His first ministry, of course, was preaching the gospel to those who had never heard it. His second ministry (second, not in importance, but in sequence) was caring for those who became believers. Pastoring follows evangelism in the spiritual order just as nurturing follows birth in the biological order.

Paul followed his evangelism with pastoral care. He established churches wherein people could be nurtured and cared for and he then kept in close touch with them. He did this by visiting and writing. His first venture into caring for his converts may have been his recom-

> **Only a nurtured and cared for church will be strong enough to continue making new disciples.**

mendation to Barnabas, "Let us go back and visit the brothers [and sisters] in all the towns where we preached the word of the Lord and see how they are doing" (Acts 15:36).

Even though Paul and Barnabas split over a disagreement about a third traveling companion, the record shows that Paul, accompanied now by Silas, "went through Syria and Cilicia, strengthening the churches" (v. 41). He was bringing the Great Charter into balance with the Great Commission.

Acts 20, as we discovered previously, tells of Paul's visit with the elders of the Church in Ephesus. His single focus was on caring for the people:

- Keep watch over all the flock;
- The Holy Spirit has made you overseers;
- Be shepherds of the Church of God; and
- Help the weak.

Not a word is mentioned about making additional disciples. His strategy must have been that only a nurtured and cared for church will be strong enough to continue making new disciples. Visiting people was one way he cared for them.

Paul also pastored by writing. He exposed his soul to the Church in

Philippi by telling them he remembered them and prayed for them (see Phil. 1:4). He assured them that he had them in his heart (see 1:7). He counseled the church in Colossae to clothe themselves with compassion, kindness, humility, gentleness, forgiveness and love. Giving counsel is a pastoral act.

To the Thessalonians Paul revealed his love. Not only did he share the gospel with the Thessalonians, he also shared his very life because "they became so dear to him" (1 Thess. 2:8). What a pastor! What care! Finally, a pastoral benediction: "May the Lord of peace himself give you peace at all times and in every way. The Lord be with all of you" (2 Thess. 3:16). Notice that these words are addressed exclusively to Christians and do not contain any reference to witnessing or evangelizing.

The record of Paul's pastoring initiatives makes our case for the Great Charter. Paul accepted responsibility for the care of the people who had become Christians through his preaching.

Tom Parrish is one of a growing number of second Reformation pastors striking a balance between the Great Commission and the Great Charter. Tom is senior pastor of the Vision of Glory Lutheran Church in Plymouth, Minnesota, a suburb of Minneapolis.

In the final chapter of my book, *Can the Pastor Do It Alone?*, Tom Parrish told his story of starting the Lay Pastors Ministry in his first pastorate, Bethel Lutheran Church, Bellbrook, Ohio.

The church was experiencing significant growth for a "small" church. Tom's concern for the pastoral care of former and new members alike compelled him to implement the Lay Pastors Ministry. I had the privilege of equipping the church's first lay pastors. It flourished and met the need.

His call to be the senior pastor of Trinity Lutheran Church of Minnehaha Falls, Minneapolis, Minnesota, left Bethel without vocational pastoral leadership for 18 months. The volunteer pastors did the pastoral care of the congregation. Fourteen years and three pastors later, laypeople are continuing to provide pastoral care.

Shortly after arriving at Trinity, Tom began laying the foundation for what proved to be an effective lay pastoral care ministry.

Tom is now pastor of Vision of Glory Church. As the spiritual leader of the congregation, he is leading his people on two parallel tracks: rapid membership growth and pastoral care. They are presently planning a new building to accommodate the growth and will soon hold their first lay pastors training seminar. They are seriously and equally committed to both the Great Commission and the Great Charter.

Hear Tom's testimony about his three-church experience with one of the two parallel tracks, pastoral care: "After 18 years of ordained ministry I do not know of any other approach to congregational care that comes close to the effectiveness, efficiency and fulfillment of the priesthood of all believers than the Lay Pastors Ministry."

Let's reflect again on the imagery of the two mighty rivers. Both waters are joined as one in the great Atlantic Ocean, just as the two mighty rivers of the New Testament—*the Great Commission* and *the Great Charter*—are joined as one in the ocean of God's great love.

A more apt metaphor at this point may be the two great mountains on the island of Hawaii, Mauna Loa and Mauna Kea. I saw them daily for the seven years I was the pastor of Haili Church in Hilo. They appear to be two separate 14,000-foot formations. They are separate; their peaks are many miles apart. But they are also joined together as one, rising to their lofty heights from a common base, the whole island of Hawaii.

In the same way, the Great Commission and the Great Charter, though they are two separate ministries, rise to their lofty heights from a common source: the massive love of God—love for the world and love for His people. What God has joined together, the Church ought not to put asunder.

But the Church is splitting the Great Commission and the Great Charter. Some churches are majoring in one and some in the other, not realizing that both are equally called forth by God. Others are ineffective in doing both. The reality is that great numbers of churches are not honoring the Great Charter. And they never will be able to honor it as long as *The Pastor* is the only pastor in the congregation.

But when pastorally-gifted laypeople are affirmed, equipped and given the ministry, the Great Charter will be honored. All of God's people will then have pastoral care. Bring your church into balance.

"He who has an ear, let him hear what the Spirit says to the churches." Do both the Great Commission and the Great Charter.

A
Biblical Church

"WHOEVER PRACTICES AND TEACHES THESE COMMANDS WILL BE CALLED GREAT."

—Matthew 5:19

"I have been saying in recent days that maybe, just maybe, God designed a truly biblical Church. Maybe He designed it to be led by leaders and taught by teachers and administrated by administrators and shepherded by shepherds. Is that a possibility in your thinking?" So spoke Bill Hybels at The Church in the Twenty-First Century conference sponsored by Leadership Network in 1991.[1]

My first assignment in seminary was to write a paper about "The Source and Norm of Theology." Two words summarize my paper: the Bible. God's holy Word is the *source* of what we believe and the *norm* by which we appraise our behavior. In other words, the Bible is our reliable guide for faith and practice.

The church in which the Lay Pastors Ministry can happen is the church that hears God by knowing, believing and practicing biblical truths. It is a Word-driven church. The Bible, however, is not a Christian idol; it is the medium through which God reveals Himself and His will to His people.

Jesus' barbed response to the Sadducees' trick question in Matthew

22:23-32 applies to many twentieth-century church leaders: "You are in error because you do not know the Scriptures or the power of God" (v. 29).

Two Scriptures that many leaders seem to be unfamiliar with are Ephesians 4:11,12, instructing pastors to equip God's people to do ministry, and 1 Peter 5:1-4, charging laypeople to pastorally care for God's people.

The ancient error of the Sadducees is the modern error of leaders who build on the same sands of tradition, reason and arrogance. They perpetuate the *tradition* that the pastor's role is to do ministry while the people's role is to receive ministry. They *reason* that the best handbook for church life and growth is written by credentialed people whose studies and programs are based on tradition. Their *arrogance* makes them unaware of their delusion, comfortable with the status quo and resistant to a paradigm shift. They have "paradigm paralysis," the inability to break out of ingrained patterns of thinking and acting.

This error explains why the expenditure of human resources, energy and money continue without corresponding results. It also explains the frustration, disillusionment, anger and burnout of so many vocational ministers.

The good news, however, is that an ever-increasing number of church leaders are seeking the guidance and inspiration of the Scriptures. They are experiencing the truth of Hebrews 4:12: "The word of God is living and active." It works!

During one of my first trips to Nassau, Bahamas, to conduct a Lay Pastors Equipping Seminar, the bishop of the Anglican Church told me, "If our people can see that it is in the Bible and if they can understand it, they will do it." That is what I call "biblical."

Seeing that lay pastoral care is in the Bible is the key to having it happen in your church. To be a biblical church is to be participating in the second Reformation: giving the ministry to the people. It is to experience what Isaiah meant by his prophecy, "See, I am doing a new thing!" (Isa. 43:19).

Let's look to three Scriptures for three pivotal truths, expecting to correct the Sadducees' error. The first is Ephesians 4:7-12, *The Pivotal Doctrine:*

But grace was given to each of us...he gave gifts....And his gifts were that some should be...pastors and teachers, [to equip] the saints [God's people] for the work of ministry (*RSV*).

The doctrine is that every Christian is a minister. Five words shine like the five points of a star to set forth this doctrine: grace, gifts, equip, saints and ministry. This doctrine fuels the second Reformation. Let's closely examine these five words:

Grace: This word means God's favor, generosity and goodness. God gives His grace in three forms: (1) salvation (see Eph. 2:8); (2) revelation (see 3:2,3); and (3) ministry (see 4:7). Grace is powerful because it saves, reveals and gives gifts for ministry.

Gifts: Many kinds of spiritual gifts have been given, and not one Christian in the whole world and in all of history has ever been overlooked. The cluster of gifts for pastoral care includes mercy, encouragement, exhortation and serving. Just as we all intend that people use the gifts we give them, God expects the same of us. We do not choose our gifts for ministry, Christ apportions them (see Eph. 4:7,8).

Equip: Preparation for ministry is an essential part of the formula. God would not think of sending His people out to do His work without adequate preparation. He has assigned pastors and teachers the task of equipping His people to do their ministries.

Saints (*Laos*, God's people): God's first call to us is to be His. Through repentance from sin and faith in Jesus Christ we are born into His family. We are no longer our own (see 1 Cor. 6:19,20). As His people, we have the privilege of access to Him and the honor of doing work for Him. We may not always behave and talk like His people, but by His grace we are.

> **Ministry:** God's second call to us is to do ministry. Ministry is some special service we do for God. Why do we resist? Moses was glad to be one of God's chosen, but when God called him to a certain task, he stubbornly resisted with some familiar reasons: not worthy, not credentialed, frightened and not competent. His final resistance was a desperate appeal to God to send someone else (see Exod. 3—4). Every Christian is a minister by virtue of the fact that God gives gifts (special abilities) to every Christian with which to do ministry and calls every Christian to a special task that utilizes those gifts. If God gives you a ministry (your special task), it follows that *you are a minister*. Many do not know this; and many who do know it are not doing it. But neither ignorance nor disobedience changes the fact that every Christian is a minister.

I have been preaching and teaching this doctrine in scores of settings for two decades, discovering again and again that it is truly *a pivotal doctrine*—the central point on which "the second Reformation" turns.

If I were the only one heralding this doctrine, or if the Lay Pastors Ministry were the only ministry laypeople were doing, my voice would never be heard. But by adding it to others, all orchestrated by God's Spirit, it is loudly resounding through the world. This sound is nothing less than the voice of the Spirit, energizing the Church with new life and energy as it moves into the twenty-first century. "He who has an ear, let him hear what the Spirit says to the churches."

The second of the three Scriptures is 1 Peter 5:2,3—*The Pivotal Charge:*

> Tend the flock of God that is your charge, not by constraint but willingly, not for shameful gain but eagerly, not as domineering over those in your charge but being examples to the flock (*RSV*).

The charge is to "tend the flock of God." The *New International Version* reads, "Be shepherds of God's flock that is under your care." This charge is pivotal because it was given to laypeople. They were elders of churches in five Roman provinces. It was true then, as it is today, that no one credentialed person or staff of credentialed people can "tend the flock" (pastorally care for all of God's people). Please note that the word *charge* is used twice. I take this to be God's way of underscoring the urgency of caring for His people.

All seven chapters in Part 1 of this book focus on this charge. It takes

> The *spirit* in which the charge [to tend the flock] is to be carried out is a spirit of willingness, not obligation; a spirit of eagerness, not greed for money.

a needs-conscious, gift-oriented, egalitarian, ministry-balanced, biblical, mobilized and failure-resistant church to pastor God's people.

As we look closely to this Scripture we observe that the charge is noticeably positioned among a cluster of other items: (1) the people, (2) the spirit, (3) the motive and (4) the payoff.

The *people* to whom the charge is given are laypeople. You can imagine who they are: shopkeepers, shippers, farmers, builders, shepherds, fishermen, wives, husbands, neighbors and other very common folk.

The *spirit* in which the charge is to be carried out is a spirit of willingness, not obligation; a spirit of eagerness, not greed for money.

The *motive* is to serve by being the best example possible, not to hold a position of power with which to lord it over others.

There is a *payoff*. For faithfully executing the charge, the laypeople will receive a crown of glory when the Chief Shepherd appears, a crown that will never fade away.

Our third Scripture is Exodus 18:13-26—*The Pivotal Model*. I call it the Mosaic model of pastoral care:

> What you are doing is not good....Select capable men...and appoint them as officials over thousands, hundreds, fifties and tens....That will make our load lighter, because they will share it with you.[2]

This model demonstrates what decentralizing pastoral care will do for both the pastor and the people. The people will receive adequate care and the pastors will have time to do what God called them to do as spiritual leaders.

Moses' father-in-law, Jethro, observed that both Moses and the people were wearing themselves out. Moses was trying to do the impossible: care for all the people himself. The people were expecting Moses to do the impossible: give personal attention to each one. It was not working.

The passage rapidly moves from the *condition* through the *solution* to the *betterment*. As I cite the following three movements almost verbatim, I invite you, my readers, to prayerfully consider where you are in the changing scenes. Every time I do this for myself, I am both affirmed and reproved. This may be the moment of paradigm shift for someone.

The Condition:
- What you are doing is not good.
- You will only wear yourself out.
- The work is too heavy for you.
- You cannot handle it alone.

The Solution:
- You must be the people's representative before God.
- Teach them.
- Show them the way to live.
- Show them the duties they are to perform.
- Select capable people; appoint them as officials over thousands, hundreds, fifties and tens; have them serve.
- Have them bring the difficult cases to you.

The Betterment:
- Your load will be lighter.
- They will share your load with you.
- You will be able to stand the strain.
- The people will be satisfied.

Whether a vocational minister or a volunteer minister, each of us is located somewhere on this continuum. From wherever we discover ourselves to be, we are challenged to take the next step; or, if we discover that we have already progressed from *the condition* through *the solution* to *the betterment,* we are challenged to strive for excellence in *the solution* scene.

I have enough faith to believe that for some readers this moment is a dramatic moment of Christian formation in your lives. "He who has an ear, let him hear what the Spirit says to the churches."

If a church is to be biblical, it must deal with the problem of mythology, for mythology grows alongside theology like tares grow alongside wheat. Mythology has the appearance of biblical theology, assumes the authority of biblical theology and is accepted as biblical theology.

A simple example of this is the Christmas story about the three wise men. Scripture simply records that Magi (traditionally *wise men*) from the east came to Jerusalem (see Matt. 2:1). Mythology numbers them (the words of one of our Christmas hymns are "We *three kings* from orient are") and, in some cases, even names them.

In a similar way mythology has grown alongside the theology of ministry! For centuries, in fact, the growth of the unbiblical myth about ministry—that only clergy are ministers—was widely accepted as biblical truth. This tare looked so much like wheat that it was (and continues to be in traditional-minded churches) substituted for the biblical teaching that all Christians are ministers.

The Church emerged from the New Testament as a "body" in which each part is given gifts for ministry and all "parts" are equally important in doing ministry. The "body" concept prevailed in every large town of the Roman Empire and to such distant places as Britain, Carthage and Persia. After Emperor Constantine legalized Christianity in A.D. 312,[3] the "body" concept was covered over.

In the centuries following, mythology flourished. It identified ministry with an office rather than a *charism.* A *charism* (Greek, pronounced kar'izum) is a special gift or power divinely conferred upon a person. Prominence, privilege and power were attributed to certain people because of their offices. The Church gradually became more an organization than an organism.

In the centuries following, mythology about ministry that has grown alongside theology these many centuries is:

- There are two classes of Christians, clergy and laity.
- The clergy are the ministers; the laity are receivers.
- A person becomes a minister by formal education and ordination.

One of the dynamics operating in this mythology is that *the people make the Church, and then the Church makes the people.* The people of that

> # When knowledge penetrates a person's spirit, attitude changes.

era made the Church hierarchical and, except for some significant variances throughout history, the Church made successive generations of churches hierarchical.

But today, "things are a changin'." The rediscovery of the pivotal theology, charge and model previously described is demythologizing the Church, giving it new life and returning it to the "body" concept. It is breaking free from its encumbrances. This is one of the most exciting times in the history of the Church!

Not all of the Church, however, is breaking free. Many individual church leaders, both clergy and laity, are not yet separating myth from truth. It is extremely difficult to break with tradition. How do we do it? How do we change?

Management consultant Ken Blanchard says that change can happen in four ways:

1. Knowledge: adding a new piece of information to your mind;
2. Attitude: changing the way you think about something;
3. Behavior: altering a habit or the way you perform a particular function; and
4. Organizational behavior: changing the way an entire group of people does something.[4]

Let's try to understand Blanchard's four ways of change.

Knowledge
The preceding pages may have added significantly to what you already knew. I trust that it has. It is said that *knowledge* is *power*. Jesus taught, "You will know the truth, and the truth will set you free" (John 8:32). Proverbs 24:5 reads, "A man [or woman] of knowledge increases strength." You have the necessary knowledge to change.

Attitude
When knowledge penetrates a person's spirit, attitude changes. Biblical knowledge about ministry shapes how pastors see themselves and how they see the people; it shapes how the people see their pastors and how they see themselves. Pastors begin to see themselves as equippers and encouragers of ministers rather than the chief doers of ministry. The people begin to see themselves as having ministries of their own, believing that they too are ministers. They experience an attitudinal change.

Behavior
Changing how we do things is very difficult because of our formal training, tradition and ecclesiastical culture. If change is to occur, it will come about by prayer and biting the bullet; we will pray, make the change, and let the chips fall where they may. Change is uncomfortable. Change puts us at risk. Change draws criticism. But change is also exhilarating, refreshing and renewing. It is the nature of everything that is alive. Changes in knowledge and attitude are significant, but nothing really changes until behavior changes.

Organizational Behavior
This is the most complex because enough of the members of a congregation have to move through the other three to change the culture of a church. People do not all move at the same time nor at the same pace, so vision, prayer, perseverance and patience are required—and in that order. Know that if corporate behavior (the culture of a church) does not change, any changes taking place are not really changes. They are only temporary, short-lived alterations that eventually revert to the way things were previously done and lead to heartbreak for those initiating them.

If you are looking for some practical, usable ideas to change your church, you will find change-power in doing the following things:

- **Create a favorable culture.** Preaching, teaching, writing, meeting and modeling contribute to creating a spiritual, emotional and rational climate. This, in turn, is conducive to successfully pursuing a vision that differs from the traditional. Culture must be defined to create a favorable lay ministry of any kind. "Culture" is that which most people in the church know is expected, permitted and appropriate. Ministries that are incongruent with the culture of a church will fail no matter how biblical, well organized, well promoted or heavily endorsed they are.[5]
- **Help people discover their ministries.** Gifts, passion, experience, personality, training and life situations all contribute to the ministry a person should be doing. Classes, seminars, workshops, publications and consultants can facilitate people in their search.
- **Create structures for ministry.** Set priorities for the church and move on them by designing ministries that will accomplish them. For most ministries, usable models already exist. By adopting or adapting them, you will not have to "reinvent the wheel."
- **Celebrate ministry.** Creative ways to focus attention on proposed ministries, new ministries, longtime ministries or just the idea of laypeople doing ministry will create a fun environment. It will help people to enjoy doing ministry. Some churches have a Sunday each year on which they recognize their "volunteer ministers." Some have an annual celebration event such as a dinner, banquet or picnic to affirm their "volunteer ministers."

"He who has an hear let him hear what the spirit says [through the Bible] to the churches!"

Notes:

1. *NEXT* (Tyler, Tex.: a publication of Leadership Network, August 1995).
2. See appendix A for two diagrams of the Mosaic Model: the first, Ministry Centralized; the second, Ministry Decentralized.
3. Bruce Shelly, *Church History in Plain Language* (Dallas, Tex.: Word Publishing, 1982), pp. 42, 108.
4. Ken Blanchard, *Forum Files* (Tyler, Tex.: Leadership Network, January 1994).
5. For a more complete treatment of "culture"—its controlling power and how to change it, I recommend R. Paul Stevens's and Phil Collins's book, *The Equipping Pastor* (Washington, D.C.: The Alban Institute, 1993), chapter III, pp. 40-56. I make additional references to the culture of a church in chapters 7 and 8. Chapter 12 tells how Paul Gilbert, pastor of Desert Hope Wesleyan Church in Phoenix, Arizona, changed the culture from the traditional belief that only ordained clergy are ministers to the biblical truth that all Christians are ministers. This change of culture enabled them to launch a successful Lay Pastors Ministry.

A Mobilized Church

EVERY MEMBER A MINISTER

It takes all the people of God to do all the work of God. I would like to see this statement become a common cliché in the Church. God's work is so important and so large that it cannot be done by the typical 20 percent of the congregation who do 80 percent of the work. Neither can it be done by paid staff. In fact, no church can hire a staff large enough to do it all. Much of God's work is left undone, even in terms of pastoral care.

A man complained through *Monday Morning,* a denominational magazine for Presbyterian clergy, about the lack of pastoral care at the time of his mother's death.[1] He told how "deeply bothered" he was. His longing for ongoing pastoral care was exacerbated by disillusionment.

A pastor's response to this complaint may seem unfairly defensive of the clergy, but he is right:

> As I understand it from Ephesians 4:11,12, God has given the gift of leaders, not to do the ministry, but to equip the saints to do *their* ministry. How might this work out in instances such as you encountered? A story of contrasts helped me understand.

First, he told of reconnecting with his former "ol' roomie" from seminary. This friend had left the ministry to enter the field of software engineering because he could no longer take the usual 10-to-14-hour days. His killer schedule was overcrowded trying to keep up with all that was going on in the lives of his people. He believed he had to be there for them 24 hours a day. In the midst of this sacrificial serving frenzy, his wife became seriously ill and was bedridden for nearly a year. Not one person from the church called or visited her.

As he shared this sad commentary about the church, "his words dripped with bitterness." The reason: "He had taught his flock that he and only he was responsible for caregiving—and they'd learned their lesson well. Too well. He soon became another casualty of the ministry."

He contrasted this by telling about what happened while he was on vacation. A major accident hospitalized a member of his church. People visited her. Some asked what they could do to help: Did she and her husband have insurance? Were meals needed? How could they pray?

Upon returning, the pastor asked the husband how he felt about the care they had received. He broke into tears while telling what the visits, hands-on help and prayers did for them. The pastor concluded with these clarifying words from Ephesians 4:11,12:

> Have I and the other pastors here responded at all hours of the day and night to emergencies? Of course. But this precious flock is willing and able to provide so much more pastoral care than we could ever dream of—and they're doing it! No, we aren't abandoning our call as pastors when we let our congregation know it isn't only *our* job to be available 24 hours a day. I think we're just learning how to fulfill that call.

THE MOSES PRINCIPLE

Moses, the leader of Israel centuries ago, gives the twentieth century Church a model for total mobilization of all God's people. Read about it in Exodus 24—30. God called him to construct a tabernacle. The only way this could be accomplished was by all the people giving materials and skills. They did it!

First, let's examine Moses' role. Every congregation has a "Moses," the central spiritual leader. This person is commonly called the pastor. Moses' role in building the tabernacle parallels the pastor's role in building a lay ministry in the following eight ways:

1. He met with God (see Exod. 24:18; 34). He entered the cloud, staying there long enough to hear God out on a variety of things, all related to the tabernacle and worship. Inwardly, he had God's plan clearly in mind. Outwardly, his face took on a radiance, so much so that he had to wear a veil when speaking with the people (see 34:29-35). This visible change signaled the people to take his words seriously because he had been with God.

Parallel Principles:

- We need a place and time to meet with God regularly.
- It is imperative that we stay with God long enough to hear Him out if our words are to have meaning and our actions are to be significant.
- The inner conviction that we have heard God generates energy, confidence, competence and integrity.
- The "something different about us" that comes from our time with God authenticates our authority to mobilize, instruct and lead His people.

2. He got his vision from God (see Exodus 25). "Vision casting" is the common term for one of the major roles of the "Moses" of a congregation. His vision was quite specific: "Have them make a sanctuary for me, and I will dwell among them. Make this tabernacle and all its furnishings exactly like the pattern I will show you" (vv. 8,9). The *vision* does not seem to be an ecstatic, other-worldly, mystical trance; it is concrete and rational. His mind must have reeled with the volume of construction details—27 pages in my Bible.

Parallel Principle:

Happy are the pastors whose meetings with God are frequent enough, long enough and deep enough to know they are hearing God, and that the vision they cast emerged during their time with Him.

3. *He taught the people* (see 35:1,4). "These are the things the Lord has commanded you to do." What he should teach the people was revealed while he was with God. The communication was so compelling that Moses knew God had spoken and that he was oligated to teach the things God had commanded.

Parallel Principle:

Teach Ephesians 4:11,12, a neglected part of God's Word, with the excitement, passion and power of a freshly given revelation: Pastors and teachers are to equip the saints to do the ministry. Then, teach the specific ministry focus of this book—pastoral care of a congregation by laypeople. Teach these as "the things the Lord has commanded you to do."

4. *He led the people* (see Exod. 33:12). Moses had no doubt that God told him to lead these people. Neither did he question that these people were God's people. His leading included providing structure for their participation in God's project. Some were to bring materials such as gold, linen and wood. Others were to use their skills in crafting metals, making curtains and braiding gold strands. Leading them included inspiring them to have willing hearts.

Parallel Principles:

- Provide structures for ministry. The Lay Pastors Ministry is a likely structure for pastoral care.
- Call all the people to use their unique giftedness to do their ministries.
- People are ready to minister when meaningfully challenged.

5. *He corrected and disciplined them* (see Exod. 32—34). Forward movement in hearing and doing God's plan was interrupted by the impatience, skepticism and idolatry of the people. This happened—it's

incredible—under the leadership of Moses' trusted associate, a priest
named Aaron. Moses had to take quick and strong action to prevent
God's plan from being derailed. The treatment was severe; their
rebellion was crushed; the people mourned; and they continued
God's project.

Parallel Principle:

> Similar threats to God-ordered ministry are common in
> today's churches. At times, the modern "Moses" will have
> to call people to be accountable lest forward movement be
> obstructed.

6. *He inspected the work* (see Exod. 39:32-43). "Moses inspected the
work and saw that they had done it just as the Lord had commanded" (v. 43). Could it be that the excellence of their work was in part the
result of knowing it would be inspected?

Parallel Principle:

> A relationship exists between quality and accountability.
> The heavy truth is that God holds his leaders accountable
> for how well (or effective) ministry is done; thus, it is
> imperative that leaders evaluate the work periodically.
> This way "in-flight corrections" can be made as necessary.

7. *He was with his people in worship* (see Exod. 40). He arranged all of
the equipment: the ark of Testimony, table, lampstands, altar, basin,
etc. He anointed the furnishings and the priests with oil. He was with
his people as the cloud covered the Tent of Meeting and the glory of
the Lord filled the tabernacle. Leading the people into God's presence
was task number one. Number two was teaching the people; number
three was mobilizing them for action.

Parallel Principle:

> Worship, teaching and mobilizing come together for us in
> Ephesians 4:1-12: "There is one God and Father of all

(worship)...but to each one of us grace has been given as Christ apportioned it....It was he who gave some to be...pastors and teachers, to prepare God's people for works of service (teaching and mobilizing)."

8. *He completed the work* (see Exod. 39:32). It reads like the end of a formal report: "So all the work on the tabernacle...was completed." The writer of Hebrews cited the reason for Moses' success: "He persevered because he saw him who is invisible" (Heb. 11:27). His frequent meetings with God kept him at it through all the discouragement and stress.

Parallel Principles:

The responsibility of pastors and all who respond to God's call is to finish the work God gave them to do, to stick with it through all the tough times and follow it through to completion. At the end of Jesus' earthly life he prayed, "I have brought you glory on earth by completing the work you gave me to do" (John 17:4). Again, Paul to Archippus: "See to it that you complete the work you have received in the Lord" (Col. 4:17). A common time-management principle applies here: It's not how much you *do*, it's how much you get *done* that counts.

One more thing must be said about this completed work. Moses completed it, but only as a building supervisor completes a project, as a coach wins so many games in a season or as a general wins the battle. It's really the people who do it. In fact, this is the only way it can be done. *It takes all the people of God to do all the work of God.* "Those who have ears, let them hear what the Spirit says to the churches."

The parallel principles in Moses' role help us to see the role of today's pastors:

- Meeting with God regularly;
- Teaching the Word from God to the people;
- Leading the people of God;
- Holding people accountable;

- Being with the people in worship;
- Completing the work.

The second role to be examined is that of the people. It is only as the people fulfill their roles that pastors are able to fulfill their roles. Football illustrates this:

It is only as the players play well that the coach is able to coach well. By each doing his part well, the team plays a good game. The role of the *volunteer* minister fits hand-in-glove with the role of the *vocational* minister:

- Meet with God regularly;
- Hear God through His Word;
- Accept the leadership of the leaders and offer your own;
- Bring your spiritual gifts and energies to the Lord;
- Worship;
- Expect inspection;
- Complete the work.

God's role is the third role we must examine. Surprised? Does this come as an afterthought? Perhaps. We often get so caught up in doing our thing that we forget God is also doing His thing. The fact is that if it were not for His role, our work would be for naught. Jesus understood this: "My father is always at his work to this very day, and I, too, am working...the Son can do nothing by himself" (John 5:17,19).

What did God do?

1. *He met with Moses.* It was God who took the initiative, descending to the top of Mount Sinai and calling Moses to meet with Him there. "So Moses went up" (Exod. 19:20). He could have refused God's initiative, but he didn't!

2. *He gave the vision.* "And let them make Me a sanctuary, that I may dwell among them" (25:8, *NKJV*). He followed the big idea of a sanctuary with the details—the size and material for the ark (acacia wood and gold), the lampstands made of hammered gold, 10 curtains of finely twisted linen, and blue, purple and scarlet yarn as well as hundreds of other details.

3. *He Himself was the motive.* "Motive" means "spring of action." The people knew God was worthy of the very best they had to give,

whether skills or materials. It was neither Moses, nor the nation, nor the project, nor their religion that moved them to give themselves to this massive task. It was God who moved them. "To the Israelites the glory of the Lord looked like a consuming fire on top of the mountain" (24:17). Awesome!

4. *He moved their hearts.* In addition to personally inspiring them to action and excellence, God gave His Spirit to form willing hearts and generous spirits. God's Spirit also bestowed "skill, ability and knowledge in all kinds of crafts" (Exod. 35:20—36:1). So, it was not only their willingness that originated with God; their competence was from God. Ours is too: "Our competence comes from God" (2 Cor. 3:5).

5. *He provided the workers.* Moses was the leader of leaders. He led in carrying out the plan that God gave him. The project leaders were Bazelel and Oholiab. They led the workers. God revealed the plan, called the leaders, gave people willing hearts and filled them all with His Spirit.

6. *He provided the materials.* The ultimate source of all things is God. He provided them; the people brought them. In fact they brought so much that Moses had to stop them from bringing more (see Exod. 36:3-7).

The tabernacle was completed. God used it immediately by filling it with His glory (see 39:32; 40:34,35). It was time to celebrate! They had heard God and acted on what they heard.

The following are a few corresponding New Testament and twentieth-century realities I mined from this model:

- *God gives the idea for lay pastoral care.*
  "Prepare God's people for works of service" (Eph. 4:12).
  "Be shepherds of God's flock" (1 Pet. 5:2).
- *Our Lord Himself is our motive for doing ministry.*
  "Surely I am with you always, to the very end of the age" (Matt. 28:20).
  "The Son of God, who loved me and gave himself for me" (Gal. 2:20).
- *God provides the material for ministry.*
  "But to each one of us grace [spiritual gifts] has been given as Christ apportioned it" (Eph. 4:7).
  "Our competency comes from God. He has made us competent as ministers" (2 Cor. 3:5,6).

- *The workers are provided by God.*
  "Ask the Lord of the harvest, therefore, to send out workers into his harvest" (Matt. 9:38).
  "You did not choose me, but I chose you and appointed you to go and bear fruit—fruit that will last" (John 15:16).
  "Each one should use whatever gift he has received to serve others, faithfully administering God's grace in its various forms" (1 Pet. 4:10).

It takes all the people of God to do all the work of God. *He who has an hear let him hear what the spirit says [through this model] to the churches!*

Commitment is the preeminent key to mobilizing a church. Earlier in this chapter, I told about the members of a church who cared for a

> Commitment assumes that the Spirit gives the gifts for doing ministry and, silently within a person's conscience, sounds the call.

woman hospitalized by an automobile accident. They were available because they were committed.

How many programs and ministries have failed because committed people were not found to do them! A pastor who delayed implementing the Lay Pastors Ministry for three years told me: "I have learned not to push a program until I have gifted and called people to do it."

By *gifted* and *called*, this pastor was talking about two essential components of commitment. Commitment assumes that the Spirit gives the gifts for doing ministry and, silently within a person's conscience, sounds the call. Mobilization gives commitment the opportunity to surface.

The reality is that not every Christian is committed. This can make mobilization extremely difficult, if not impossible. In fact, the rule of thumb is the 80/20 rule: 80 percent of the work gets done by 20 percent of the people. What could your church do with 50 percent of your people working; or, to dream wildly, 75 percent working?

That a high percentage may be only a dream is documented in a formal study of seminaries, churches and pastors:

> Lay members, despite fairly regular attendance by about half of the population, are generally ill-informed about the basic tenets of their faith, often *lukewarm in their commitment* (italics mine) to building a community of believers devoted to serving Christ with passion, urgency and abandon.[2]

Marginal commitment, which creates great difficulty in achieving ministry objectives, is an issue churches have to deal with. This is especially true in light of shrinking budgets for staff and increasingly less discretionary time for members.

Some churches are reaping the ministry benefits from strengthening the commitment component of their cultures. One such church is the First Evangelical Church in Memphis, Tennessee. Pastor Duane Litfin tells about it:

"We emphasize 'one member, one ministry.' If you ask one of our members, 'What's your ministry?' he should be able to answer....When you say, 'I want to join this church,' that is a statement of commitment. So, for members, I expect attendance at worship, close relationships and active ministry. One of our strategic goals is that by the year 2000 every member will be in some form of ministry."

His reply to the question, "Do people know these expectations when they join?" was, "Yes, the 'every member in ministry' is in our Target 2000 strategic plan. And in the new members' class, I'm up front about the expectations."[3]

Another church where commitment is a strong component of its culture is the Frazer Memorial United Methodist Church in Montgomery, Alabama. They are able to identify 5,000 of their members doing specific ministries. On a Sunday I worshiped with them, the congregation was asked to stand and greet one another by telling what ministry they were doing. Pastor John Ed Mathison tells in the following words how important the "every member in ministry" theme is to their church:

> The emphasis on the ministry of the laity is something that must be kept constantly before the church. An occa-

sional sermon is not sufficient. It needs to be taught in Sunday School and preached from the pulpit.

We say that each new member is expected to find some place to serve in the life of the church. That expectation level is echoed from the pulpit....People hear it often. It becomes a level of expectation.

When people join your church, they should be given immediately an opportunity to indicate where they feel led to serve.[4]

Mobilization for ministry, activated and sustained by commitment, is the engine that drives ministry. At least seven signs mark an every-member ministry church:

1. An intentional, well-defined strategy.
2. A programmatic provision to enable people to discover their gifts, to hear God's call and to come forward to commit themselves to a ministry.
3. Publicizing specific equipping opportunities and schedules.
4. A process for presenting a "menu" of ministries from which people can choose. This process replaces using delegation, appointment or election to determine where individuals should serve—"filling slots" as someone called it.
5. An every-member ministry preaching and teaching priority, thereby making the biblical teachings on spiritual gifts and divine call well known by the members.
6. Communicating the high-level expectation to new members that every member of the church will be serving God in some specific ministry.
7. Lay leaders model their every-member ministry orientation.
8. Clergy and other staff leaders relinquish ministry to gifted and equipped laypeople.
9. People are comfortable with the goal of every-member ministry—the expectations, procedures, theology and terminology—as characteristic of the culture[5] of their church.

We have seen that mobilization of the congregation is the key to ministry, and that commitment is the key to mobilization. It's time to ask, Just what is commitment?

Commitment is that compelling force within the self that drives one's decisions for action. It is generated by the simultaneous activity of the Holy Spirit and the human mobilizer—the call of the Holy Spirit being heard by a person's spiritual ear while the call of the mobilizer is being heard by the person's physical ear.

Because this commitment is deep within the person, it can be quite an emotional thing, but not necessarily so. In fact, we need to be aware of the difference between a feelings-driven assent and Holy Spirit/human spirit-driven engagement. Paraphrasing a humorous plaque I read in a novelty store helps me understand the difference: "Kissin' don't last. Cookin' do." My rendition: "Feelin's don't last. Commitment do."

Commitment, then, is that life-controlling energy deep within one's self, generated as the Holy Spirit bonds with the appeal. The Holy Spirit continually nourishes that ministry energy to the degree we continue to be "filled with the Spirit" (Eph. 5:18).

Without commitment a person may intend to do ministry, but may not follow through, just as the son said to his father, "I will, sir," when told to go work in the vineyard. But he did not go (Matt. 21:30).

Without commitment a person may do ministry for a time but not continue, like Demas who, according to Colossians 4:14 and Philemon 24 was Paul's fellow worker and "dear friend," but according to 2 Timothy 4:10, deserted Paul "because he loved this world."

When a person is committed he or she will do ministry and, though wavering at times, will continue doing it. This is Peter. He "left everything and followed him" (Luke 5:11). Though sometimes weak, he was committed. We read of Peter's continuing commitment throughout the Gospels and the book of Acts.

These three—the son, Demas and Peter—shed new light on commitment. Making a commitment is one thing; continuing a commitment is another. The act of commitment *sets* the course; acts of renewed commitment *stay* the course.

When members are weak in commitment, it is usually the church that is at fault. If the church is not strong enough to call its people to commitment and then again to renewed commitment, it will be too weak to mobilize its people for ministry. We must call our people to commitment. The energy of the Spirit will be in these calls, thereby releasing the energies of the congregation into ministry.

"He who has an ear, let him hear what the Spirit says to the churches." *Let laypeople do it!* by mobilizing your congregation.

Notes

1. *Monday Morning*, a magazine for Presbyterian leaders, P.O. Box 636, New Palentine, IN 46163 (December 18, 1995): 1-16.

2. "The M.J. Murdock Charitable Trust," Review of Graduate Theological Education in the Pacific Northwest, P.O. Box 1618, Vancouver, WA 98668.

3. *Leadership Journal*, 465 Gunderson Drive, Carol Stream, IL 60188, Summer 1989, p. 126.

4. John Ed Mathison, *Every Member in Ministry*, Discipleship Resources, P.O. Box 189, Nashville, TN 37202 (1988): 6.

5. Culture is that which most people in the church know is expected, permitted and appropriate. Ministries incongruent with the culture of a church will fail no matter how biblical, well organized, well promoted or heavily endorsed. The culture will overpower and outlast all additions and changes, returning them at the first opportunity to what was done and how it was done prior to the addition or change. For this reason, in most churches, the culture has to be changed if Every Member Ministry is to be a reality. Culture is changed by planning, preaching, teaching, modeling, practice, patience and prayer in an environment of love and respect.

A Failure-Resistant Church

"A WISE MAN BUILT...HIS HOUSE ON THE ROCK...IT DID NOT FALL."
—Matthew 7:24,25

A Kentucky pastor accepted my invitation to explain in one of my training seminars what his church was experiencing with the Lay Pastors Ministry. Two years earlier he had shared glowing reports of success and delight with its effectiveness.

He began to relate how the ministry blasted off like a rocket. Lay pastors were excited and those they pastored were grateful. His facial expression and voice changed, however, as he now told of the ministry's failure.

He proceeded to give the reasons for the failure so those attending the seminar could avoid making the same mistakes:

1. He had managed the ministry by himself;
2. He had not organized a Ministry Leadership Group;
3. Problems arose and he was too busy with other demands to deal with them.

Another church reveals a different story. Glad Tidings Church (Assemblies of God) in Lake Charles, Louisiana, started its Lay Pastors Ministry during the fall of 1990. This church saw the need of adequate care to match its steady growth. (This congregation is building a sanctuary to seat 3,500 as I write.) It was my privilege to conduct the equipping seminar for its first lay pastors.

The ministry began with considerable energy and did well for the first couple of years, but eventually leveled off and began to decline. A team of laypeople and staff attended our international conference in Montgomery, Alabama, during the spring of 1994. They sought ideas and inspiration and went home with both to restart their ministry. Today this ministry is flourishing. The senior pastor, John Bosman, has developed excellent equipping materials and has helped several area churches start a lay pastoral care ministry.

No church can have a failure-free ministry. I bought a "wrinkle-free" shirt only to discover that there is no such thing. However, it is "wrinkle resistant." Likewise, we would hope there could be a failure-free ministry. But the best we can have is a failure-resistant ministry. Only the universal and eternal Church that Jesus Christ is building is failure-free: "The gates of hades will not overcome it" (Matt. 16:18). It's the individual churches, programs and ministries, however, that come and go.

So, how can we have a *failure-resistant* ministry? First, the ministry must be meeting a need. The Lay Pastors Ministry does that. People are not always aware of their needs for pastoral care, but God is. One pastor, speaking about the lay pastoral care ministry in his church, said it this way: "We meet the needs people are aware of and many of which they are not aware until they begin to get regular pastoral care."

Because God's charge to "Be shepherds of God's flock" (1 Pet. 5:2) is for all time, we know that pastoral care will always be needed. It's how the care is packaged that may need revising from time to time. Today, grassroots pastoral care—layperson to layperson—is replacing top-down pastoral care—clergy to parishioner. The Lay Pastors Ministry is meeting a basic need.

Jesus' ministry is our model. The crowds followed Him because He addressed their needs. He met people's bad news with good news. Let's look at a few examples:

- The demon-possessed man. The bad news was that demons had taken over his life. Jesus' good news was directed to his bad news and the man became demon free.
- The 5,000 hungry people. The bad news was that they were weak from not having eaten and no food was available. Jesus' good news addressed their need. He provided food; they ate and were filled.
- The criminal. The bad news was that he was suffering capital punishment on the cross. Jesus' good news spoke to his greatest fear: "Today you will be with me in paradise" (Luke 23:43).

Bad news comes in many forms and is universal. It plagues all people in varying ways and degrees. Good news also comes in many forms and is intended for all people. It originates with God, therefore it brings hope

> Ministry leaders bear the responsibility for quality because excellence is contagious.

(good news) into hopeless situations (bad news). Like Jesus, the pastor—vocational or volunteer—can offset bad news with good, not by providing generic answers, but by providing life-producing solutions.

The second way of having a *failure-resistant* ministry is to commit to quality. Because we do the ministry in the name of Jesus Christ, we must do it correctly—from the largest task of designing the ministry to the smallest details of managing the ministry. (Have you heard that the devil is in the details?) Quality is the goal.

Engraved on the cornerstone of one of America's great churches, the Coral Ridge Presbyterian Church in Fort Lauderdale, Florida, is a commitment to quality: "Excellence in all things and all things to God's glory." Ministry leaders bear the responsibility for quality because excellence is contagious. Unfortunately, so are sloppiness, mediocrity and carelessness.

The third way to a *failure-resistant* ministry is to use what I call The Twelve Foundation Blocks.[1] I discovered these after five years of successful lay pastoral care ministry.

I was invited to a men's breakfast in Lexington, Kentucky, to tell about Lay Pastors Ministry's effectiveness. In my preparation, while reflecting on the ministry and seriously asking myself what made it successful, the following 12 components surfaced.

You will find that The Twelve Foundation Blocks provide a solid base for beginning a ministry. They can also be used as evaluative instruments to expose possible weaknesses for established ministries. Corrective action can then be taken before the ministry begins to decline.

Although they are listed as a series, these 12 blocks are one unit and should be treated as a whole. Ministry health is a unity of many contributing factors in the same way physical health is a unity of many contributing factors.

Cardiologist James Rippe's wisdom regarding physical health illustrates the importance of considering The Twelve Foundation Blocks as a unit: "Fitness is not just one quality of life. It's really *a unity of many contributing factors*...spiritual, mental and physical health fit together"[2] (italics mine).

My paraphrase of his statement: "Effective ministry is not achieved by drawing on just one or two elements. It's a unity of many contributing factors: vision, ownership, design and the other foundation blocks. Each one is essential to the sturdiness of the ministry."

FOUNDATION BLOCK 1: VISION

"Where there is no vision the people perish" (Prov. 29:18, *Amp. O.T.*). Vision can be defined as "Something seen by other than normal sight." When asked how she could bear to live with blindness, Helen Keller said that it is far worse to have sight without vision. Envisioning what this ministry will mean to the members of the church (the "flock of God") and to the spiritual leader (the "Moses") of the congregation is essential.

- **A Biblical Base and Call: 1 Peter 5:1-4.** "Tend the flock of God that is your charge" (v. 2, *RSV*) is both the biblical

base and the call of God to church leaders to see that every last one of their people is loved and cared for.
- **Needs of the Congregation.** Reviewing the membership list is all it takes to document the need for pastoral care.
- **Prayer.** Time spent with God in prayer will keep the vision bright and alive.
- **Shared with Leaders.** Common vision creates unity and focus.

FOUNDATION BLOCK 2: OWNERSHIP

Someone has to "own" the ministry; that is, someone must be responsible for it, manage it and be accountable for its effectiveness. This requires a Ministry Leadership Group of 4 to 15 people (depending upon the size of the church) who share the vision and assume the responsibility.

- **Commissioned by the Pastor and Official Board.** Lay pastors need to be released into ministry through prayer and the laying on of hands. Doing so will establish the members of the leadership group as partners with the vocational pastor in fulfilling the Lord's charge to "Tend the flock."
- **The Priority Ministry for Each in the Group.** This is not a ministry people can add to what they are already doing in the church. Some will need to drop other commitments to focus on this.
- **Some Signs of Ownership:** Attending meetings regularly; thinking about the ministry at times other than during the meetings; talking about the ministry at home, with friends and in other settings; agonizing over the problems (even losing sleep over them); exhilarated by progress and successes.

FOUNDATION BLOCK 3: DESIGN

An adequate organizational structure is as important to ministry as the skeletal structure is to the human body. The purpose needs to be clearly stated and the goals written. "Wherever the grace of Christ is present, it is in search of a form that will adequately express what it is," wrote Avery Dulles in *Models of The Church*.³

The design is used in launching the ministry in the same way a blueprint is used in building a building.

- **Determine Purpose and Goals.** Our stated purpose is to provide pastoral care for every household. The acronym "SAM" provides the imperative for goals: Goals must be Specific, Achievable and Measurable.
- **Create an Adequate Structure.** Organizational structure must be seen as indispensable to your ministry.
- **Develop Job Descriptions.** Determine who is to do what, then put the "what" into writing.
- **Build upon All Twelve Foundation Blocks.** Each building block is important. It may take several months to get your ministry tracking this way; but when you do, it will endure.

FOUNDATION BLOCK 4: CALL

"You did not choose me, but I chose you" (John 15:16). Laypeople seldom think of themselves as being called by God to a ministry. Thus the local shepherd must teach the flock to hear the voice of the Shepherd, so each one can do what he or she has been called to do.

- **Accept Spiritual Giftedness and Divine Call as Essentials for Those Who Participate.** The call to ministry is included in our call to salvation. The Bible makes it clear that everyone in the Body—every Christian—is given gifts for ministry. The Holy Spirit, then, enables each of us to discover whether we are an ear, an arm or an eye.
- **Confirm the Call of Each Participant.** Not every person wanting to be a lay pastor is gifted or suited for this ministry. It is vital that a lay pastor's call be authenticated by (1) himself or herself, (2) the ministry leaders and (3) the church leadership.
- **Provide for Public Recognition and Acceptance.** At a Sunday morning worship service we have a special time

for laying on of hands by the elders, setting them apart for this ministry.

FOUNDATION BLOCK 5: EQUIPPING

"Equip the saints for the work of ministry" (Eph. 4:12, *RSV*). The *New International Version* says it another way: "Prepare God's people for works of service."

- **Adopt the Biblical Requirement of Equipping.** Equipping enables one to minister with confidence and competence. There are three equippers: (1) people (see Eph. 4:11,12); (2) the Holy Spirit (see Acts 1:8); and (3) the Scriptures (see 2 Tim. 3:16,17).
- **Design a Course.** Determine the subjects in which your lay pastoral caregivers need to be equipped. Two areas must be researched: equipping them to *be*; and equipping them to *do*. My book *Can the Pastor Do It Alone?* includes 12 units for equipping, all that lay pastors need to get started ("basic training").[4]
- **Identify and Enlist the Equippers.** According to Ephesians, pastors and teachers are to equip God's people for ministry. In 2 Timothy 2:2 we discover the next phase: Pastors are to equip other people to be equippers.
- **Provide Ongoing Equipping.** This can be formal or informal. It can be done in hour-long, half-day, whole-day workshops or weekend retreats.

FOUNDATION BLOCK 6: ACCOUNTABILITY

"It's not what is *expected* that gets done, it's what is *inspected*," says a former colleague of mine.

Experience has shown that when accountability lapses, the acts of ministry decline. Accountability has to be built into the ministry. The Lay Pastors Ministry does this in three major ways: monthly reports, pastoral supervision and ministry-sharing times.

- **Provide Reporting Forms, Policies and Procedures.** The

ministry Leadership Group needs to determine what they
will do regarding reports, setting the policies and implementing them. Feedback is imperative!

- **Pastoral Supervision.** Each lay pastor has a lay pastor. The
first responsibility of this person is to pastor the lay pastor.
The second is supervision. The question, Tell me, how is
your ministry going? expedites the process.[5]
- **Sharing About the Ministry in a Small Group.** Our lay
pastors meet regularly. During each meeting they divide
into small groups of 5 to 10 to share with one another what
they are doing, how they are feeling about it and expressing their agonies and ecstasies. They never think of sharing as a time of accountability, but it is.

FOUNDATION BLOCK 7: AFFIRMATION

Words of encouragement and appreciation with a pat on the back
ignite the spirit. Affirming people is biblical. Romans 13:7 exhorts us
to "Give everyone what you owe him...if respect, then respect; if
honor, then honor."

- **Give Public Recognition.** Some ways this can be done are
by articles and pictures in the church papers, posters on
the walls and affirmations from the pulpit.
- **Plan an Annual Ministry Celebration and Recognition
Event.** Some churches have an annual "Ministry Celebration
Dinner." Honor and recognition keep us from growing weary
in our well-doing and give us a sense of accomplishment.
- **One-on-One Affirmation.** Occasional notes, cards, letters
or phone calls to recognize faithful ministry are excellent
means of affirmation.

FOUNDATION BLOCK 8: SUPPORT

"Many persons can do most of what we pastors do....The task of pastors is to equip these persons for ministry and *support* them through
administration and example."[6]

We vocational pastors are notorious for getting people to volunteer for tasks and then leaving them high and dry. They need support and we need to give it.

- **Availability of Staff and Leadership.** The pastor, or pastoral staff, needs to be available to deal with problems and answer questions.
- **Arrange for Prayer Partners.** The desire and will is there. All that is needed is to provide some plan for them to pray for one another.
- **Pastoral Supervision.** For them to know that they have someone who is praying for them, who is interested in them and who will be meeting with them regularly gives strong support.

FOUNDATION BLOCK 9: FELLOWSHIP

The community that ministry creates must come together for sharing, renewing and growth. All who minister must be able to move from ministry to community; then from community back into ministry.

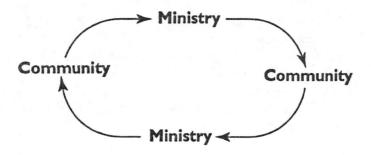

Our regular meetings, called "Lay Pastors Connection," have five components: worship, ministry news, equipping, sharing and fellowship.

- **Plan Social Events.** Creativity is the key. Socializing makes ministry fun and bonds people together. Annual picnics, Christmas parties and other events provide the breeding ground for friendship to be cultivated. Some people are attracted to a ministry because of the fellowship.

FOUNDATION BLOCK 10: COMMUNICATION

The ministry cannot be strong without frequent verbal and printed contact.

- **A Monthly Newsletter.** It should equip and inform. Our newsletter is one 8½x11 sheet, both sides.[7]
- **Church Paper Articles.** The lay pastoral care ministry must be highly visible to the congregation for two reasons:

1. You will need to be calling people from the congregation into the ministry; and
2. The people will accept lay pastors more readily because of the ministry's visibility.

- **Special Mailings.** Occasionally special mailings can be used to accentuate some milestone in the ministry or some special event.
- **Personal Witness at Worship Services.** A good three-point sharing outline can be:

1. What I am doing?
2. Why I am doing it?
3. How do I feel about it, or what is this ministry doing for me personally?

- **Be in Touch with Other Churches and the Network.** This can be done by exchanging newsletters, speakers, publications, etc. Keeping in touch with the international network is also mutually beneficial.[8]

FOUNDATION BLOCK 11: EVALUATION

Taking time to see how the ministry is doing will keep it moving ahead. This can be done by asking the questions:

1. Are we doing what we set out to do?
2. Are we having the results we projected?
3. Are we using the methods and means we planned to use?
4. Do we need to make some changes? If so, what?

Evaluation assumes that we have a stated purpose, goals and objectives against which we can measure the current state of the ministry.

- **Design Instruments for Evaluating the Ministry.** This may take some special help from someone experienced in this skill. Or adapt evaluation forms from other organizations. Do at least one evaluation a year.
- **Utilize the Results for Ministry Improvement.** The hard work begins after the forms are returned. They need to be collated, interpreted and used to affirm, correct or change the ministry.

FOUNDATION BLOCK 12: MAINTENANCE

This is the nuts and bolts of day-to-day office and administrative work. Unless the maintenance is done, the ministry will break down sooner or later.

- **Do Essential Office Work.** Keeping records, processing reports and publishing and distributing the newsletter are a few examples of this work.
- **Keep Watch over the Flocks Regularly.** The size of the pastoring groups will diminish because people move away, transfer to other churches or die. Unless the number of people in the flocks are reviewed regularly, the total being pastored will decrease.
- **Provide Materials.** Materials must be gathered for workshops, equipping seminars, monthly meetings and other events.
- **Review and Update the Structure, Policy and Participants.** This is the task of the group that has ownership of the ministry. If the ministry is alive, it will be changing.

The Twelve Foundation Blocks cause us to personalize the words Jesus spoke in the Upper Room: "Now that you know these things, you will be blessed if *you* do them" (John 13:17, italics mine). Do them and you will be blessed!

"He who has an ear, let him hear what the Spirit says to the churches." Do your work well because it is your Lord's work.

Notes:

1. The complete copy of *The Twelve Foundation Blocks*, a 14-page *Monograph by Mel*, is available from Lay Pastors Ministry, Inc., 7132 Portland Avenue, Minneapolis, MN 55423.

2. Quoted from a review of the book, *Fit Over Forty*, by Dr. James Rippe in the *Saint Paul Pioneer Press*, (May 30, 1996): p. 2-B.

3. Avery Dulles, *Models of the Church* (New York: Doubleday, 1974), p. 66.

4. Melvin J. Steinbron, *Can the Pastor Do It Alone?* (Ventura, Calif.: Regal Books, 1987), pp. 93-124. These 12 units are also on videocassettes, *A Complete Lay Pastors Equipping Seminar*. When used with the accompanying guide, it makes an 8- to 12-hour equipping seminar. The book and videotapes are available from Lay Pastors Ministry, Inc.

5. A more complete explanation of Pastoral Supervision can be found in *Can the Pastor Do It Alone?* (Ventura, Calif.: Regal Books, 1987), pp. 71-78.

6. Samuel Southard, *Comprehensive Pastoral Care* (Valley Forge, Penn.: Judson Press, 1975), p. 7.

7. A sample of Hope Church's monthly newsletter, *Keeping PACE*, is available from Lay Pastors Ministry, Inc.

8. There is a network of churches in the United States, Canada and Australia. They publish a quarterly newsletter, sponsor an annual conference on lay pastoral care and distribute resources. Contact them through the Lay Pastors Ministry, Inc.

PART II:
What Kind of People Does It Take?

Conclusions:
The Kind of Church
It Takes

GETTING FROM HERE TO THERE

As I began to write the conclusions about the kind of church it takes, I was interrupted by a phone call from a church that had previously contacted me about starting the Lay Pastors Ministry. They had decided to delay the ministry until the congregation had completed a gift and ministry-discovery adventure. "People who are to do pastoral care need to get some idea about their gifts and have a sense of call," the person explained. They were absolutely right!

These church leaders, having identified pastoral care as their priority need, plan to lay the foundation for an effective and lasting ministry rather than rush to the front with a hastily-put-together Band-Aid program. Their plan allows time to incorporate all seven of the qualities delineated in the preceding chapters. These qualities are hallmarks, not only of lay pastoral care, but also of every form of effective and lasting lay ministry.

The following is a brief review of the seven qualities:

Needs-Conscious: Awareness of the need for pastoral care.
Gift-Oriented: Focusing on spiritual gifts by preaching, studying and using gift-assessment helps.

Mobilized: Creating a "ministry-friendly" environment for volunteer ministers by concentrating on laypeople doing ministry.

Ministry-Balanced: Committing to *the Great Charter* as well as *the Great Commission*.

Egalitarian: Entrusting the grass-roots ministry of pastoral care to laypeople will transform the split-level church into a one-level body of believers. The title "Minister" will now be related to gifts and call rather than office.

Biblical: Accepting 1 Peter 5:2, *RSV* ("Tend the flock"), Ephesians 4:11,12 ("[Equip] the saints for the work of ministry," *NKJV*) and other Scripture as words from God.

Failure-Resistant: Taking time to do things right to increase the probability of success.

DEVELOPING THE SEVEN QUALITIES FOR SUCCESSFUL LAY MINISTRY

How do you go about developing those qualities? The question really is How do you change a church? We get some helpful insights from management consultant Ken Blanchard, who has been a consultant and trainer for Chevron, Lockheed, AT&T and other major corporations. *Leadership Journal* met with him in his offices in Escondido, California, to find out how church leaders can create lasting, effective change:

1. *Change is difficult.* "It's tough enough to start a church, but it's murder to turn one around. Do you know how long it will take to make a major change in the way your church operates? Anywhere from two to five years of concentrated effort, depending on the size and complexity of the organization."

2. *The person at the top has to have a clear vision.* "Moses didn't go up the hill with a committee; if he had, he would never have come down. My advice to ministers: be clear about the vision."

   It is important to find out what the congregation wants. "But notice," Blanchard said, "this is second." The congregation usually does not have the large picture. The goal is to get the vision of the congregation and the vision of the pastor to match.

3. *Be willing to work.* Blanchard quotes famed football coach, Don Shula: "I've won more games because I'm willing to roll up my sleeves and do whatever it takes to make it happen."

Blanchard continues, "Sure, it's coming up with the vision and the direction, but then the vision must be implemented: coaching, supporting, giving direction, praising, progress and redirecting."

He expands the willingness to work principle: "But

> ## "Leadership is more of a partnership; unless the follower is willing to follow, you don't have much leadership."
> ## —Ken Blanchard

vision alone can't get it done. Too often we spend all our time on vision and none on implementation. At some point, you've got to move."

He points to Jesus as the model for this active involvement. In fact, he told Peters and Waterman, who wrote *In Search of Excellence*, "You didn't invent management by wandering around. Jesus did."

He obviously sees in clergy and other leaders a relationship between willingness to work and ego: "Managing the journey of change is servant leadership. We must get our egos out of the way and praise, redirect, reprimand—anything it takes to help people win." (Someone defined *ego* by using the letters to make an acronym: Edging God Out.)

4. *Know where the people are.* Leaders (vocational and volunteer) cannot just announce a change and expect people to support it. Until people have their first-layer concerns

answered (What is this and why? Where am I going to fit? How will it be done? What is the impact?) they are not likely to be open to the change.[1]

Wise leaders are beginning to believe that leadership is not something you do *to* people, it's something you do *with* them. Blanchard reports: "Leadership is more of a partnership; unless the follower is willing to follow, you don't have much leadership."

> To affect an individual's *will*, you must know where the person is and journey with him or her from that point.

The old rhyme applies: "A person convinced against his will remains unconvinced still." To affect an individual's *will*, you must know where the person is and journey with him or her from that point.

If change is to take place, a systemic view of the church is essential, i.e., seeing the church as a system. Paul Stevens and Phil Collins make this clear in their book, *The Equipping Pastor*: "Change takes place when it is not merely programmatic but *on the level of the church's systemic life and through a process consistent with its systemic life*" (italics theirs).[2] They give their reason for this conviction: "Every church has a corporate 'feeling' that communicates to new and old members what is important and what is permitted." By *corporate feeling* Stevens and Collins mean *culture*.

To grasp Stevens's and Collins's idea, we need some common understanding of the two words, *systemic* and *culture*. *Systemic* means the inter-relatedness of every part of the church, so much so that when one part changes, all other parts change. Visualizing the church as a mobile helps understand the church as a system.

Culture can be conceptualized as the "genetic code" of the church, determining what new members and successive generations consider valuable, right and proper. In most churches, culture is the unresearched and unrecognized dynamic that drives the church. A former colleague of mine in Cincinnati, Dr. Gary Sweeten, maintained that if you want to find out how something in the church works, try to change it. The hue and cry will tell you.

Every church is a *system* and has a *culture*. To know all you can about both informs you where you have to start in making changes. For example: If the members believe that the ordained clergy person is the only person qualified to do pastoral care, the "Moses" will need to connect with the members where they are if he or she expects to turn pastoral care ministry over to the people. The members will need to journey from where they are to the biblical truth that they, too, are bona fide (i.e., genuine, without fraud) *ministers*. For many, this will be a long and difficult journey, but it is the way to *let laypeople do it*. To make this journey together is to help people hear what the Spirit is saying to the churches.

In the next chapter we will focus on the person Ken Blanchard calls "the person at the top," the vocational minister. We'll consider what kind of pastor it takes for lay ministry to happen in a church.

Note: The Lab for these eight chapters can be found in appendix B.

Notes:
1. Ken Blanchard, *Leadership Journal* (Spring 1996), 114-118, adapted.
2. R. Paul Stevens and Phil Collins, *The Equipping Pastor* (Washington, D.C.: The Alban Institute, 1993), p. 45. If you desire an in-depth treatment of system and culture, I recommend this book.

What Kind of Pastor Does It Take?

MOSES: OUR PROTOTYPE FOR LETTING LAYPEOPLE DO IT

Writing this chapter has caused me to feel like Moses at the burning bush (see Exod. 3—4):

"Who am I that I should do this?"

"What if they do not believe me or listen to me?"

"I am slow of speech and tongue."

"O Lord, please get someone else to do it."

God gave Moses to Israel. In spite of his inadequacy and resistance, God protected his life at birth, rescued him from the Nile, attracted him to the burning bush and called him to lead His people.

God provides every congregation with a "Moses" to whom He gives the same call He gave to Moses:

1. Journey with My people. Bring them from where they are to where I want them;
2. Teach them My decrees and laws and the duties they are to perform;
3. Select, appoint and train capable people who fear God;

4. Have them bring the difficult cases to you;
5. They will share the ministry with you;
6. You will be for Me a kingdom of priests.[1]

Moses made the one great mistake clergy have been making throughout the years: he tried to keep the ministry to himself. I say, "tried." Actually, he *did* keep the ministry to himself, but it didn't work because of the nature of ministry—ministry is to be shared. Jethro's counsel (read Exod. 18:17ff) to Moses is well suited for leaders today:

> What you are doing is not good! It is too much for you and you are depriving the people of their ministries. Listen to me and may God be with you—decentralize!

Clergy, we have our ministry; laypeople have theirs. Let them do it. Jethro's counsel amplifies the message of this book, *let laypeople do it!* In his book *The Disciple-Making Pastor,* Bill Hull gives "Let laypeople do it" as one of the six steps expressing Jesus' teaching method.[2] Jesus came to the time in training His disciples when He sent the Twelve out on their first mission without Him. They were on their own. He is our model for letting laypeople do it.

LEADERS SPEAK OUT

I have heard there is safety in numbers; therefore, I invite you to listen with me to what some of the finest leaders in the field of pastoring and pastoral care are saying:

> JOHN PATTON, professor of Pastoral Theology, Columbia Theological Seminary, Decatur, Georgia, and adjunct professor of Pastoral Care, Candler School of Theology, Emory University, Atlanta: "[I view] clergy as 'generalists' in ministry, representatives of the 'whole' ministry of the community of faith, whereas the laity are more often than not 'specialists' in a particular type of ministry, such as...the ministry of pastoral care."[3]

PAUL STEVENS, academic dean of Regent College,

Vancouver, British Columbia, and associate professor of Lay Theology and Empowerment: "It is helpful to think of pastor and laity as *co-pastors* of a church and co-equippers....Equipping the laity is not mobilizing the laity to help the pastor but helping people discover and develop their own ministries."[4]

WILLIAM EASUM, director of 21st Century Strategies, Inc., who formerly led Colonial Hills United Methodist Church of San Antonio, Texas, in unprecedented growth: "Pastors that have a need to be needed in order to find validation for their ministries will have a hard time giving up control of the actual ministry to the congregation. Pastors who need to keep laity dependent on them will avoid these forms of ministry....Pastors who are interested only in maintaining the status quo will not do well with [lay pastoral care] ministry."[5]

JOHN ED MATHISON, senior pastor of the Frazer Memorial United Methodist Church, Montgomery, Alabama, one of the fastest growing United Methodist Churches in America (83 percent of the resident members are involved in a specific area of ministry): "Part of our problem in stagnant churches today is that many people have a mind-set that ministry is to be done by the clergy and professional staff....The implication is that professional people are hired to do ministry and laypersons within the church are the recipients of that ministry....This misconception must be corrected! The biblical message is that every member of the church should be involved in ministry."[6]

PETER WAGNER, professor of Church Growth at Fuller Theological Seminary School of World Missions, an authority in the field of church growth: "If clergy can believe that their primary role is that of equipper and if the laypeople will give their consent and open the way for their pastor to be such a person, churches can grow both in quantity and quality."[7]

LOREN MEAD, founder of the Alban Institute, an Episcopal priest with many years in parish ministry: "The church of the future must break the power of clericalism (the church's power system)....Clergy by themselves cannot and will not relinquish their power. There will be no change until the laity takes the lead. The church is too important to be left in the hands of the clergy."[8]

OSCAR E. FEUCHT, a Lutheran (Missouri Synod) pastor, churchman and theologian whose writing reached me at a formative time in my ministry and impacted me more in the areas of lay ministry than any other at that time: "Consider the changes necessary if the church is to become what God intended it to be: A ministerium of *all* who have Christ in their hearts....Whoever has the gospel has also a ministry."[9]

Spencer Christian, the "Good Morning America" meteorologist, concludes the national weather, "That's what's happening on the national scene; here's what's happening where you are."

Let's paraphrase Spencer's transitional statement, "We've just read what leaders across the nation are doing and saying; now let's see what's happening where you are." Regardless of the good "weather" at Colonial Hills UMC in San Antonio, Texas, and Frazer Memorial UMC in Montgomery, Alabama, you are responsible as the "Moses" of your congregation for what is happening where you are.

All the meteorologist at the local station can do is report; he or she can't do a thing about the weather. But we can do more than report what's happening in our churches; we can do something about it. We can move the seven qualities in Part I from print to practice. In fact, God holds us accountable to do it.

THREE ESSENTIALS FOR PASTORS: VISION, ACTION AND SUPPORT

The kind of pastor it takes will have the *vision*, take the *action* and give the *support* required for authentic and effective lay ministry to happen. Having said this, I could close the chapter; but we need to spend some time with each of these three essentials.

Vision

"Church leadership must provide vision, and while recognizing the inevitable tension between vision and reality, never allow the vision to shrink down to the level of reality." This philosophy guides Kirbyjon Caldwell, the senior pastor of Windsor Village United Methodist Church in Houston, Texas.[10] We should all be immersed in this kind of respect for vision.

My experience of being temporarily lost provides a good illustration of vision. While taking a walk in Northern Minnesota, I took what I thought would be a shorter route through the woods back to the resort where I was staying. I had walked beyond sight of the road and other familiar markers, and there was no path to follow. I became disoriented. The sun which could have given me direction was eclipsed by clouds. Turning to the right and then to the left to avoid troublesome undergrowth only took me farther off course. I had no idea where I was or in what direction I was going. Fear belted me. I shouted, "I think I'm lost!"

Even though I could not see where I was, a helicopter flying overhead could have easily seen *who I was*—a resident at the resort; *where I was*—about 800 feet into the woods; and *where I should be going*—by turning right and continuing north I could have walked out of the woods. The pilot would have had *vision*, the ability to see (1) who I am; (2) where I am; and (3) where I am going.

Nehemiah is an example of one who had vision:

- *He knew who he was*—a man upon whom God had placed His hand and in whose heart God had put what he was to do for Jerusalem.
- *He knew where he was*—in Babylon, far from where he needed to be.
- *He knew where he was going*—to Jerusalem to survey the ruins and mobilize the Jews to rebuild the city.

For one whom God has called to be the pastor of a church, vision is to ministry what life is to the body. A church in Sussex, England, inscribed on its wall: "A vision without a task is but a dream; a task without a vision is drudgery; a vision and a task is the hope of the world."

So just what is meant by *vision*? Vision is the ability to imagine and prepare for the future. It is the power (or act) of perceiving abstract or invisible subjects as clearly as if they were visible objects. The *Concise Oxford Dictionary* defines it as imaginative insight, statesmanlike foresight, sagacity in planning.

But vision is more than that. It seems to have a life of its own. Vision is that persuasive revelatory assignment from God, to which we give our lives and for which we work with all our hearts.

I heard David Yonggi Cho from Seoul, Korea, the pastor of the largest church in the world, say, "You will not make the vision, the vision will make you." He assumes that God gives the vision. He started with only five people to preach to, but when he closed his eyes he could see 3,000. His congregation now numbers more than 500,000. Such is the power of vision.

Possessing a vision (or perhaps I should say *being possessed by a vision*) assumes a personal relationship with God, a sincere commitment of one's life and ministry to God, a continuing conversation with God, obedience to the Scriptures and a strong desire to fulfill a call from God in God's way.

Vision keeps us staying the course when the going is difficult. Samuel Zwemer paints a graphic picture of this in *Call to Prayer:*

> The Alpine climber who is trying to reach the summit can, on the upward path, scarcely see his goal except at certain fortunate moments. What he *does* see is the strong path that must be trodden, the rocks and precipices to be avoided, the unbending slopes that become even steeper. He feels the growing weakness, the solitude and the burden. And yet, the inspiration of the climber is the sight of the goal. Because of it, all the hardships of the journey count for naught.[11]

The supreme importance of vision for ministry is underscored by hearing about the importance of vision for corporate life. John Naisbitt wrote in *Re-inventing the Corporation*, "The company's vision becomes a catalytic force, an organizing principle for everything that the people in the corporation do."[12]

> **Vision channels energies by enabling everyone to point the same direction.**

I have taped these words on the panel of my word processor so I see them every time I write. I want them etched deeply in my being. Vision is power...power to do God's work! And the part of God's work we are focusing on in this book is the pastoral care of God's people: "Tend the flock of God."

Vision enables the "Moses" of a congregation to persevere with God's call to his people. If Moses had listened to his congregation and appeased them, they would have returned to Egypt and bondage. Never would they have arrived in the Promised Land! Pastors who

> # Vision should unite,
> ## not divide the church.

give their congregations only what they want are seldom able to lead their people to new heights. We must go to the mountain often to refresh the vision, renew the energy and stay on course.

What if the manager of the Minnesota Twins baseball team did what the people want? For example, they want him to yank the pitcher because the Seattle Mariners have batted around and there is still only one out. The fans have vision, but it's *short-term* vision. They want to shut off the runs. The manager also has vision, but his is a *long-term vision*. He sees that letting the pitcher get out of this jam will develop him into a good pitcher for next season. The manager sees the larger picture.

These two kinds of vision clash. Mutual love and respect between laity and clergy, long-range strategic plans, conflict-management skills and lots of prayer will be necessary to "keep the unity of the

Spirit through the bond of peace" (Eph. 4:3). Vision should unite, not divide the church.

Most people do not see the larger picture because it is usually not a part of their calls. But the pastor must. He or she needs to see both the smaller and larger picture, with the smaller giving way to the larger when necessary. A conference ad read: "The senior pastor is the one who is responsible to secure a vision from God that is so overwhelming that he knows it could not have come from his own mind."

This does not mean that the pastor is the only one with vision. When the vision originates with another, if the pastor believes it is from God, he or she has to "buy into" it, because it is the pastor who will lead the congregation in its acceptance and implementation. Such is the nature of pastoral authority and leadership.

The following six steps may help pastors to assess the vision and move it into action:

1. In an unhurried and prayerful moment, close your eyes for a time of silence.
2. Meditate upon these questions, remembering that the focus may become clear only after repeated times of silence throughout several days or weeks:
   • *What is God calling my church to be?*
   • *What is my part in making this happen?*
   • *What are my people to be and do?*
3. This is your vision, your "imaginative insight." Seal it in your spirit with prayer. Write it down.
4. As soon as it's appropriate, share it with other leaders and/or friends.
5. If they confirm it, proceed to "cast the vision," as it is called. Formally present it to the official board for processing and by teaching and preaching it to the congregation. Remember: "Vision channels energies by enabling everyone to point in the same direction."
6. Give leadership to programming it and to mobilizing the people.

These six steps have already carried us into the second essential, *action*.

Action

When I was young in the ministry, still "wet behind the ears," reading about translating vision into reality usually generated a queasy feeling. Not because I didn't believe in it, but because I *did* believe in it and therefore would have to do it. The "dis-ease" was caused by anxiety and fear. Fear because I had no training in how to do it; anxiety because I would have to change my whole ministry orientation from clergy-centered to lay-centered. I was trained in the clergy-centered model to preach the Word and to do ministry. That was it. And, sad to say, according to studies that have been made, that continues to be *it* for clergy being trained today.[13]

It was easier to be traditional, to stick with preaching the Word and doing the ministry. Occasional pricks of conscience, followed by surges of frustration, rattled my cage from time to time; but mostly I was comfortable in the traditional seminary-cast mold. My people were not asking for more; they also were very comfortable in their tradition-cast mold. They hired me to do the ministry and I was earning my salary.

I didn't know until years later what I had been missing by failing to translate my preaching *about* lay ministry into action. Worse than that, I didn't know I was cheating my people by not giving the ministry to them. And, even far worse, I was delinquent in my divine call.

"Just do it!" How many times you have heard and seen this Nike ad? God is saying the same. I, for one, need to hear it regularly because one of my negative habits is procrastination—putting things off to a more convenient time. The Spirit of God must have targeted me as a likely subject in whom He would build *action now*, because throughout a long period of time I had a steady diet of *do* in my morning times with God. The message seemed to cascade from every Scripture I read. See what a few of them do for you:

Whatever he *does* prospers (Ps. 1:3, italics mine). If you have ever received a letter from me, the last line reads, "May God prosper all you do." Such is the impact these four words have made on my life.

Do not merely listen to the word, and so deceive yourselves. *Do* what it says (Jas. 1:22, italics mine).

You see that his [Abraham's] faith and his actions were working together, and his faith was made complete by what he *did* (2:22, italics mine).

Now that you know these things, you will be blessed if you *do* them. (John 13:17, italics mine).

But as for you [Mel] (I wrote my name in my Bible before the comma), be strong and do not give up, for *your work* will be rewarded" (2 Chron. 15:7, italics mine).

The message from the Bible is simple, clear and powerful: *God will prosper what we do, not what we don't do.* The specific *doing* we are talking about on these pages is giving the grassroots, one-on-one pastoral care ministry to the people. *Let laypeople do it!* We have the vision. If we will act, the vision of laypeople pastorally caring for the members of the church will become reality.

We learn great things about carrying vision forward to visible form via action by reading the first chapters of Nehemiah. Nehemiah's invisible concern moves through action to newly-built visible walls. The year is 445 B.C. Nehemiah is in Susa, the capitol of Babylon, held captive with hundreds of other Jews. Jerusalem, 750 miles away, lies in ruins.

Upon hearing a report of the city's desolation, Nehemiah sat down, wept, fasted and prayed. In this time of deep anguish, God gave him the vision to rebuild the city. He was consumed with a passion to change a discouraging scene into a beautiful, secure and thriving city.

He moved the vision ahead by asking Artaxerxes, king of Babylon, for permission to go to Judah to rebuild Jerusalem. Upon his arrival, he surveyed the city, confirming that it was indeed in ruins. Then he shared his vision with the priests, the officials and "the rest of the people [who were to do the work]" (Neh. 4:19).

His next act was to mobilize the people by issuing a call: "You see the trouble we are in: Jerusalem lies in ruins and its gates have been burned with fire. Come, let us rebuild the wall of Jerusalem, and we will no longer be in disgrace" (2:17).

Can you visualize an informed and concerned pastor consumed with passion for changing a discouraging pastoral scene into a beautiful well-cared-for congregation? His vision has been processed through the necessary channels and the people are being mobilized: "You see the trouble we are in; many of our members struggle alone with their problems because there is no one to care for them. Come, be equipped as lay pastors and help fulfill God's call to 'tend the flock.'"

Through his action, Nehemiah's vision—"the abstract, invisible subject"—was taking visible form. The people said, "Let us start rebuilding" (v. 18). They came together; the walls went up. Nehemiah had promised, "The God of heaven will give us success" (v. 20) and He did!

Have you been doing what I did as I reread this exciting adventure? Did you compare Nehemiah's journey from vision to reality with your own? Your passion for a lay pastors ministry may still be in the vision phase, or even in the prevision phase of awareness for the need of your people for pastoral care. You have become troubled by the condition and are praying about it. God is giving you the vision. Or, already having the vision (or the vision having you), you may be formulating plans in your spirit, bringing others into your confidence, getting formal approval (just as Nehemiah did, first from the king and then from the Jews), issuing the call and starting the ministry.

It may be helpful to retrace Nehemiah's steps so each one of us can see where we are on the continuum from vision to reality:

1. Aware of the need (1:3).
2. Troubled by the condition (1:4).
3. Fasting and talking with God about it (1:4,5).
4. First action step: articulating the vision to another (2:5).
5. Second action step: doing the necessary things to get started (2:11-18).
6. Third action step: casting the vision (2:17,18).
7. Fourth action step: getting the people's response (2:18).
8. Fifth action step: beginning the project (2:18). Note that Nehemiah did not try to do it alone.
9. Reassurance that the vision was from God. "The gracious hand of my God was upon me" (2:8,18). "God had put [it] in my heart" (2:12). "The God of heaven will give us success" (2:20).

Now that you have pegged where you are on the continuum, hear Jesus: "Now that you know these things, blessed are you if you *do* them." And in a broader sense, hear again the refrain from Revelation: "He who has an ear, let him hear what the Spirit says to the churches." If the Spirit leads, take time now to:

- See who you are;
- See where you are; and
- See where you are going.

Some basic elements to action need to be considered. One is *entrust*. Just as both God and Paul entrusted the pastoral ministry to Timothy ("Timothy, guard what has been entrusted to your care," 1 Tim. 6:20), pastors must trust laypeople with ministry. The following story shows how one pastor entrusted ministry to a layperson:

For eight years, Bob Radatz and I frequently breakfasted together to talk about Hope Church's deacon ministry. It's important to get the whole picture: Bob is a layman, making his living refinishing furniture and painting. I am a member of the pastoral staff with special responsibility for the deacons.

One morning I said, "Bob, I have a word from the Lord for you." He grinned. I handed him a scrap of paper on which I had paraphrased the words of Paul to Timothy, "Bob, guard what has been entrusted to your care."

Throughout the years it became progressively clearer that Bob was to be entrusted with the deacons ministry. He had gradually moved into doing what I as a staff member was doing, leading the deacons ministry. It was an interesting process—one which I recommend to all clergy. As he moved step by step into more ownership, I moved step by step out of active participation.[14] Under Bob's leadership, the deacons have increased their ministries to 12, with a ministry leader for each. Entrusting this important ministry to Bob made it "his ministry," releasing his creativity and energy to lead the deacons far beyond where I could have led them.

Entrusting, of course, assumes giftedness, call and equipping. It also assumes *support*, the third essential we will be discussing.

Now, however, let's move on to the next basic part of action, *legitimize*. The pastor is a "legitimator" (I think I've just coined a word!). The members of the congregation often project their feelings about God onto the clergy. A member of the church can encourage another, but in most cases only the pastor can give meaningful permission. Remember: The pastor is the "Moses" of the congregation. In words familiar to all of us, "If the top person is not behind it, it's not going anywhere."

Another basic part of action is *relinquishing*. If the pastor does not relinquish ministry when it becomes apparent that laypeople are ready to accept it, the vision for giving the ministry to the people will never become reality. I know of a committed and competent layman who wanted to keep his pastor from "working himself into the grave." He offered to visit the people in nursing homes weekly. The

> # Relinquishing frees;
> # delegation freezes.

pastor accepted his offer (without relinquishing it). After several months of faithful ministry, the man discovered that he was not reducing the pastor's crushing load because the pastor continued his same visiting schedule. You guessed it—the man quit.

What I did with Bob Radatz is called *relinquishing ministry*. I must confess that the process was more intuitional than intentional. Only as I look back over the years am I able to see what I was doing. Now, knowing what was happening, I am in a position to do it intentionally with others.

Three cautions: first, don't pass off abdication of responsibility for relinquishment. Giving ministry to people too soon will frustrate them and result in failure. We clergy walk a narrow line between illegitimately skipping out of a ministry, leaving laypeople "high and dry," and timely relinquishment.

Second, don't confuse delegation with relinquishment. When you delegate, you retain ownership, expecting the person to do the work "as it ought to be done."

Howard Bell, president of Churches Alive![15], tells of correcting a man who bore a major responsibility under his overall direction. He felt the man was not following the prescribed way of doing things. "Howard," the man said, "you better make up your mind whether or not you have confidence in me. If you do, then get out of the way and let me show you how I can get the right things accomplished in the way I operate best." Relinquishing frees; delegation freezes.

Third, some laypeople misunderstand relinquishing ministry (or giving the ministry to the people) as laziness, shirking your job, gold-bricking or "nothing more than getting someone else to do what you don't want to do." Pastors, we have to be prepared for this criticism because this charge reveals what relinquishing ministry looks like to those not biblically oriented. And, unfortunately, that is what it *is* for some few clergy.

The following story demonstrates how one pastor, Vic Winquist, publicly relinquished the grassroots pastoral care of his congregation to the 38 people being equipped to receive it. Vic is the pastor of the Spring Lake Park Baptist Church in Spring Lake Park, Minnesota (a suburb of Minneapolis), where I had the privilege of giving the equipping seminar. As I frequently do, I asked the pastor to spend 10 to 15 minutes explaining to the new lay pastors what this ministry would mean to him and to his congregation.

He told them about his daughter who refused to allow anyone to take care of her newborn daughter. One evening, however, she and her husband needed to attend an event to which they could not take the infant. Reluctantly, this new mother phoned the grandmother, Vic's wife, to ask if she would care for her baby. That evening Vic's daughter brought the precious bundle to their home, carefully placed it into the grandmother's arms and slowly retreated out the door.

In solemn tones and with moist eyes Vic told the people, "For the years I have been here, pastoral care has been my baby. Today I am handing this baby over to you." Before he sat down, he added, "One more thing, I expect one of you to be my lay pastor."

This took place four years ago and, at the time of this writing, their Lay Pastors Ministry continues to provide basic pastoral care for every household of the congregation.

Now that we've moved from *vision* to *action*, let's turn to what it takes to sustain the action. First, it takes *authority*.

A pastor has authority, but it is a derived authority. All authority comes from God and we are accountable to Him for its use, disuse and misuse. Part of the nature of authority is that we have to reach out and claim it. It does not automatically come with the pastoral role.

Authority also comes from the people who recognize pastors as spiritual leaders and look to them for guidance. If the people do not give pastors authority, pastors do not have it. One indication of people withholding authority is refusing to take the pastor seriously, not believing in him.

As with all the spiritual gifts, God gives authority to be used. Hebrews 13:17 is awesome: "Obey your leaders and submit to their authority. They keep watch over you as men [and women] who must give an account. Obey them so that their work will be a joy, not a burden, for that would be of no advantage to you."

As we've already seen, part of the nature of authority is that you have to reach out and claim it. In the United Methodist ordination service, the bishop says to each person ordained, "Take thou authority." The bishop doesn't bestow authority, but offers it to be claimed. If any pastor fails to claim it, he won't have it—not by design, but by default. You have it; use it!

Authority is sometimes erroneously thought of as power. Power relies on credentials, position or force to get a job done. Authority relies on persuasion, integrity, respect and the worthiness of the effort to get a job done. We have the same kind of authority Jesus had, the kind that inspires people to take us seriously because of our love, servant spirits, selflessness, integrity and truth. The scribes had power, but when people heard Jesus, they "were amazed at his teaching because he taught as one who had authority, and not as their teachers of the law" (Matt. 7:28,29).

Occasionally, a pastor will abuse his or her authority. The consequences are serious. Some abuses are:

1. Making decisions without consulting the people who are affected by them.
2. Introducing changes or new policies without the group or person who is responsible for its implementation being in on the formulation.
3. Failing to acknowledge good work done; carelessly failing to affirm people.

4. Not being available to support people when they are in trouble or struggling with their ministries.
5. Wanting to maintain a hold on everything, or at least keep a finger in the pie.
6. Taking the credit for what others have done.

Laypeople also have authority, but they will claim it only when the pastor relinquishes it. Just as pastors have authority over their Moseslike ministry, laypeople are to have authority over their ministries. Until laypeople cease projecting authority for their ministries onto the pastor, they will not be able to function on their own. The pastor must come to the place where he or she refuses to be the authority for people doing their ministries.

Action is also sustained by *courage*. It takes courage to begin moving from vision to reality, and it takes a steady flow of courage to continue. Courage is required to break with tradition. Courage is necessary to call people, not only to commitment to Jesus Christ as Lord and Savior, but also to call them to commitment to ministry. Preaching about it is not enough.

It takes courage to call your people to accountability, to rebuke, correct, discipline or deny when necessary, and to do it in love. Because you have a Moseslike ministry, you will often feel a Moseslike loneliness. The reason is that many times you *are* alone.

It also takes *patience*. Just as a rose will be destroyed by prematurely opening the petals, so too, lay ministry requires right timing. A pastor, out of enthusiasm for starting the Lay Pastors Ministry in his church, scheduled me for an equipping seminar. He had to cancel because people did not register. He was discouraged. But my counsel to him was to consider starting at square one with his people, preaching and teaching about spiritual gifts and God's call to every Christian.

Perseverance is also crucial to sustaining action: keeping at keeping at it. The Scriptures prod us: "You need to *persevere* so that when you have done the will of God, you will receive what he has promised" (Heb. 10:36, italics mine); and "Let us run with *perseverance* the race marked out for us" (12:1, italics mine).

The bottom line to sustaining action is *hard work*. Taking authority and using it is hard work. Courage is hard work. Patience is exhausting. Perseverance will wear you out. Some covet a leadership role but are not ready for the "blood, sweat and tears."

The year I participated in Robert Schuller's annual Institute for Successful Church Leadership (I gave Lay Pastors Ministry work-shops), Dr. Schuller gave six autobiographical statements about success in leadership:

1. I don't know how to succeed in a hurry.
2. I don't know how to succeed alone.
3. I don't know how to succeed painlessly.
4. I don't know how to succeed aimlessly.
5. I don't know how to succeed permanently.
6. I don't know how to succeed without sensitivity to human need.

Each one separately spells H A R D   W O R K.
Together they spell C O N T I N U O U S   H A R D   W O R K.

Sometimes I feel like Tevye in *Fiddler on the Roof:* "God, if we are your chosen people, would you mind choosing somebody else for a while?"

My pathetic cry is a paraphrase, "God, if you have called me to do this ministry, would you mind calling somebody else for a while?" It's hard work! But God provides adequate strength to go the distance.

Success in ministry and Jesus' words, "Well done, good and faithful servant!" (Matt. 25:21) are adequate compensation.

Support

A third essential for the kind of pastor it takes to have a Lay Pastors Ministry is *support*. Volunteer ministers are not like the battery-oper-ated rabbit we see in the TV ad that "just keeps going and going and going." They need the support of their spiritual leader, the vocational minister. They need him or her to encourage them and to help them out of trouble when they get in over their heads—to have a watchful interest and concern without trying to control. Briefly stated, one of the main tasks of the vocational minister is to help laypeople succeed in their ministries.

Included in *support* are: affirmation, nurture, assistance and advo-cacy. A relationship of love and trust will enable the pastor to fulfill this part of the shepherding role without paternalistic overtones. A few simple but powerful ways of giving support and building that relationship are (1) on-the-job visits, (2) well-timed phone calls and (3) written notes and/or faxes.

In this chapter we have looked at the three essentials for the kind of pastor it takes to have a lay pastoral care ministry in his or her church: vision, action and support. Before we move on, I feel I should sound a warning: Watch out for *inertia* and *homeostasis*.

Inertia is the tendency of a person at rest to remain in a state of rest. Most people have difficulty getting going. This is especially true when vision is still only a vision, and action has not yet been taken. It's too easy to remain inert. Scripture exhorts, "Discharge all the duties of your ministry" (2 Tim. 4:5).

Homeostasis is the springlike action that returns an object to its former state. In changing the culture of a church or keeping a ministry going, a person must constantly resist the power to revert to previous practice. Again, Scripture prods, (Paul to Archippus) "See to it that you complete the work you have received in the Lord" (Col. 4:17).

"He who has an ear, let him hear what the Spirit says to the churches." Pastors, let laypeople do it!

Note: For a Lab on this chapter, see appendix C.

Notes:

1. Exodus 2 and 3. An in-depth study of this passage should yield a unique message to you from God regarding your ministry.
2. Bill Hull, *The Disciple-Making Pastor* (Old Tappen, N.J.: Fleming H. Revell, 1988) p. 190.
3. John Patton, *Pastoral Care in Context* (Louisville, Ky.: Westminister/John Knox Press, 1993) p. 8.
4. Paul Stevens and Phil Collins, *The Equipping Pastor* (Washington, D.C.: The Alban Institute, 1993) pp. xxiii, 34.
5. William Easum, *Dancing With Dinosaurs* (Nashville, Tenn.: Discipleship Resources, 1983) p. 77.
6. John Ed Mathison, *Every Member in Ministry* (Nashville, Tenn.: Discipleship Resources, 1988) pp. 1,2.

7. C. Peter Wagner, *Leading Your Church to Growth* (Ventura, Calif.: Regal Books, 1984) p. 79.

8. Loren Mead, *The Once and Future Church* (Washington, D.C.: The Alban Institute, 1994) pp. 95-97.

9. Oscar E. Feucht, *Everyone A Minister* (St. Louis, Mo. Concordia Publishing House, 1974) pp. 8,51.

10. Kirbyjon Caldwell, "Jesus as the New Paradigm," *Forum Files* (August 1994).

11. Quoted by Rowland Croucher, *Rivers in the Desert* (Sutherland, NSW, Australia: Albatross Books, 1991) p. 115.

12. Ibid., p. 113.

13. The M.J. Murdock Charitable Trust (Vancouver, Wash.) commissioned a Review of Graduate Theological Education in the Pacific Northwest. The "Preview Copy" was printed in 1994. One summary paragraph reads: "Most pastors believe they were well prepared for their pastoral duties of teaching and preaching. But, they believe they were not prepared in the areas of leadership,...development of lay leadership or the ability to withstand the rigors of leadership. In some cases, there is almost an attitude of resentment toward the seminary because of what the pastors sense was lacking in their education. Many pastors said they left seminary with tools for preaching but had to find other sources to learn needed leadership skills...and this made them less effective than they wanted to be." Among the proposals for "The Model Seminary" was to teach spiritual gifts and how to use them, and inspiring persons to do what God calls them to do.

14. Op.Cit., (Stevens and Collins), pp. 64-69, 156. "Active Participation" is one of four styles of leadership taught by Paul Stevens and Phil Collins. A pastor is to move from that style to "Passive Participation," which is being sort of a safety net for the committed and competent layperson who has moved to the "Active Participation" quadrant. A graph illustrating the four styles and a full definition of them are in chapter 4 of their book. My ministry style has been impacted by this book.

15. Churches Alive! Address: Box 3800, San Bernardino, CA 92413.

What Kind of Person Does It Take?

DO WHAT YOU CAN, WITH WHAT YOU HAVE, WHERE YOU ARE

I once saw a cartoon of a man standing in shoulder-high snow trying to shovel his way free. The caption read, "Do what you can, with what you have, where you are." This caption not only fits the man shoveling the shoulder-deep Minnesota snow, it also fits a person pondering and praying about being a lay pastor; or a person who has taken the training and is ready to make the first contact.

It fits church leaders (vocational and volunteer) whose task it is to enlist, equip and deploy lay pastors. They are looking, not for ideal people (they do not exist), but for real people, *people who do what they can with what they have where they are.*

As we have clearly seen, lay pastors are making a difference in the lives of members of hundreds of churches. What kind of people are these lay pastors? What kind of person does it take?

THINK *DIRECTION*

The kind of person it takes to do pastoral care is one who thinks *direction*, not *perfection*. Direction is what Jesus looked for in disciples: people who were willing to follow Him.

He alone is *perfection*. Like you and me, the disciples were faulty. But their direction was faultless; they followed Him!

Jesus never gave up on His disciples no matter how imperfect they were because they continued to go in the right direction. I found the following imperfections recorded in Matthew's Gospel:

1. On five occasions, Jesus told them they had "little faith" (Matt. 6:30; 8:26; 14:31; 16:8; 17:20).
2. He had to rebuke and correct them often (16:23; 19:13,14; 20:22,23).
3. After teaching them for three years He asked, "Are you still so dull?"; and later, "Do you still not understand?" (15:16; 16:9).
4. At a crucial time, Jesus found them sleeping and asked, "Could you men not keep watch with me for one hour?" (26:40).
5. Mark reports that they were jealous with selfish ambition, arguing about who among them was the greatest (see Mark 9:34).

You and I can identify with these flaws, right? But Jesus does not reject us because of them.

One of the Twelve disqualified himself—Judas, not because he was imperfect, but because he reversed direction. So, when you ponder your suitability for significant ministry, think *direction*, not *perfection*. As a follower of Jesus, you qualify!

Jesus saw more of the disciples' faults than they did, but He also saw more of their potential. Peter and Andrew saw themselves as fishers of fish; Jesus saw them as fishers of men. Matthew saw himself as a tax collector; Jesus saw Matthew as a people collector. No matter how you see yourself, Jesus sees you as a minister, perhaps a lay pastor who will care for some of His people. He looks beyond your faults and sees your potential.

Jesus renamed Simon "Peter," which means "rock." But Peter was not a rock at that time, and he was still not a well-formed rock three years later. Jesus enlisted Peter because He saw what Peter would become with Jesus' presence, teaching and Spirit at work in his life. He was far from perfect, far from being fully ready for ministry; but he was headed toward it. Again, as you ponder whether you are the kind of person it takes to do this ministry, think *direction*—following Jesus—not *perfection*.

As you read through this chapter, learning more and more about the kind of person it takes to give pastoral care, know that if you have responded to Jesus' call, or are ready to respond, you qualify. You are ready to do significant and effective ministry.

Doing ministry with competence and confidence is a lifelong, ongoing, ever-perfecting process for all of us. From a purely human perspective, the disciples were not the right kind of people to carry on Jesus' mission. I have no idea who wrote the following "Open Letter," but I have used it to communicate to thousands in my seminars that it is Jesus' call, and that alone, which qualifies us to minister for Him.

To: Jesus, Son of Joseph
Woodcrafters Carpenter Shop
Nazareth 25922

Dear Sir:

Thank you for submitting the resumés of the twelve men you have picked for management positions in your new organization. All of them have now taken our battery of tests. We have not only run the results through the computer, but also arranged personal interviews for each of them with our psychologist and vocational aptitude consultant.

The profiles of all tests are enclosed. You will want to study each of them carefully.

As part of our service and for your guidance, we make some general comments. These are given as a result of staff consultation and come without any additional fee.

It is the staff's opinion that most of your nominees are lacking in background, education and vocational aptitude for the type of enterprise you are undertaking. They do not have a team concept. We recommend that you continue your search for persons of experience in managerial ability and proven capability.

Simon Peter is emotionally unstable and given to fits of temper. Andrew has absolutely no leadership qualities. The two brothers, James and John, the sons of Zebedee, place personal interest above company loyalty. Thomas demonstrates a questioning attitude that would tend to undermine morale. We believe it is our duty to tell you that Matthew has been blacklisted by the Greater Jerusalem Better Business Bureau. James, the son of Alphaeus, and Thaddaeus definitely have radical leanings. They both registered a high score on the manic-depressive scale.

One of the candidates, however, shows great potential. He is a man of ability and resourcefulness, meets people well, has a keen business mind and has contacts in high places. He is highly motivated, ambitious and responsible. We recommend Judas Iscariot as your controller and right-hand man. We wish you every success in your new venture.

Sincerely yours,

Jordan Management Consultants
Jerusalem 26544

A *PASSION* TO DO MINISTRY

"Why are you doing it?"

The question was being asked of three people doing pastoral care ministry in our church. Their answers were for the benefit of new recruits. One responded, "I have received so much from people in the church. I *wanted* to give something back."

Another, "I really *wanted* to be a lay pastor for a long time before I became one, but I had to straighten out some things in my life first."

The third, "When I first heard about the chance to make a difference in people's lives, I *wanted* to do it."

Wanted is the common denominator.

Bruce Bugbee, in *Networking*, calls this common denominator *passion*.[1] *Passion* is where your heart is. Call, gifts and *passion* converge. Any one of them may take the lead in helping an individual discover his or her specific ministry. What kind of person does it take to do this ministry? One who *wants*—has the desire, the passion—to do it.

Passion for the ministry gives birth to commitment. A lay pastor's fundamental commitment must be to Jesus Christ as Savior and Lord. The designation, Savior, is central to salvation. The designation, Lord, is central to ministry.

Jesus taught commitment to His 12 disciples:

> If anyone would come after me, he must deny himself and take up his cross and follow me (Mark 8:34).

> No one who puts his hand to the plow and looks back is fit for service in the kingdom of God (Luke 9:62).

> Whoever serves me must follow me; and where I am, my servant also will be (John 12:26).

All the churches in our network ask their lay pastors (sometimes called "shepherds," "lay ministers," "care partners," etc.) to commit themselves to P A C E. This acronym is the job description for people who give pastoral care. (See page 4 in the introduction of this book as well as pages 63 through 66 in my book *Can the Pastor Do It Alone?*[2] for a detailed explanation of P A C E). The lay pastors must make a commitment to be faithful in *Praying* for their 5 to 10 households, being *Available* to them, *Contacting* them and being an *Example* for them.

Other commitments we ask of our lay pastors are:

1. Commitment of time and energy;
2. Commitment of years, as long as the Lord leads;
3. Commitment to continue being equipped;
4. Commitment to accountability;
5. Commitment to the church and its leaders;
6. Commitment to the regular meetings of lay pastors.

Commitment is essential, first to the Lord; second, to the church (ministry organization and leaders); and third, to the 5 to 10 households. The Lay Pastors Ministry promises to P A C E the members of the church. If this promise is not matched by the commitment of the lay pastors, the ministry will lose integrity.

THE PHASES OF COMMITMENT

Wanting (or passion) to be a lay pastor must pass through the *decision* phase on its way to *commitment*. Marriage illustrates the course. A man has an interest in a certain woman; he finds her attractive, delightful and charming. Her mystique and personality hold his interest. The chemistry is right; he feels comfortable with her. He moves on to a decision. He wants her for his wife; he pops the question. The answer is yes. Now for the commitment, the marriage.

With this example in mind, it is easy to understand the transition from wanting to be a lay pastor through the decision phase and on to commitment. The layperson finds the ministry attractive, delightful and charming. He or she can see possibilities in being a lay pastor. To stop at this point is to be like Hank and Lucille who courted for 20 years. Lucille, on a warm moonlit night, asked Hank if he didn't think it was time they get married. "Sure, but who would have us?" was his puzzling reply. If there is to be a marriage, the relationship has to move beyond wanting. However, wanting will always be a part of the marriage.

The same is true for ministry. The initial passion is in perpetual need of rekindling. The "flame" of Timothy's pastoring must have flickered because Paul wrote, "fan into flame the gift of God" (2 Tim. 1:6). He also had to remind the Christians in Rome, "Never be lacking in zeal, but keep your spiritual fervor, serving the Lord" (Rom. 12:11). The desire must always be there.

What kind of person does it take to be a lay pastor? One who has a passion to do it, a man or woman whose wanting metamorphoses into commitment.

FIVE ELEMENTS OF COMMITMENT TO THE LAY PASTORS MINISTRY

Commitment generates the energy to do ministry, and the core of commitment includes five elements.

Action

The first is *action*. God has promised to prosper what we do, not what we don't do. Psalm 1:3 reads, "whatever he *does* prospers" (italics mine).

Jesus concluded the Sermon on the Mount with an emphasis upon doing: "Everyone who hears these words of mine and *puts them into practice* is like a wise man" (Matt. 7:24, italics mine). Know that everything you do, even the least significant, such as giving a cup of cold water, will be carried to great heights of effectiveness by God.

One of baseball's greats, Matt Williams, third baseman for the San Francisco Giants (at least at this writing), said of his sport, "Baseball is a great game. I love to play it; but I can't watch it. It's boring." This is also true about ministry; there is more joy in doing than watching.

Maturity

The second element is *maturity*, or maturing (the process is ongoing). Commitment moves us in the direction of maturity. Some do not believe they are mature enough to be lay pastors, but commitment, not maturity, is the entrance-level requirement. Commitment, which is a process, not a fixed state, carries us forward to greater maturity. I'm not talking about age, how long a person has been a Christian or how experienced he or she is in Christian living. I'm talking about growing, about the process of maturing.

> Owning the ministry does not warrant ignoring the leadership of the pastor any more than playing the violin warrants ignoring the leadership of the conductor.

How mature was Peter when Jesus told him, "Take care of my sheep" (see John 21:16,17)? How many of the 72 (see Luke 10:1,17) were mature when Jesus sent them out? How many of the Twelve (see Mark 6:7)? Not many. But they were all committed, and they were all growing in maturity.

Acknowledging Leadership

The third element is *acknowledging leadership*. You move from passive participation in the life of the church to active involvement when you make a commitment to be a lay pastor. Someone compared this radical change to moving out of the symphony audience, picking up the violin, and beginning to make music yourself.

The ministry is yours! Owning the ministry, however, does not warrant ignoring the leadership of the pastor any more than playing the violin warrants ignoring the leadership of the conductor.

Leadership is of God. Leaders furnish vision, unity, direction and vitality. This is not a ministry for mavericks, but for those who will work "hand in glove" with the leaders.

You Will Have to Do It

If not you, then who? The fourth element is believing that if pastoring is going to get done, *you will have to do it.* Vocational ministers have neither the time nor the energy; and in many cases, neither the inclination nor the spiritual gifts to care for everyone. More often than not their hearts are only with people in a general or overall sense. The lay pastor, however, is there in a specific and continuing sense.

The vocational minister can be compared with the manager of a baseball team. He relies on the players, the pitching coach, batting coach, first base coach, trainer, equipment manager, scouts and others. He cares about the players and the others in an overall sense. His best energies, however, are given to strategy, morale and public relations. Can you imagine what would happen to him, to the team and to the fans if he tried to do it all? If pastoral care is going to happen in a church, the "players" (volunteer ministers) will have to do it.

The *Pastoral* and the *Care* of "Pastoral Care"

The final elements of commitment are the *pastoral* and the *care* of "pastoral care." What makes care *pastoral*? Jesus gives the answer:

> I tell you the truth, anyone who gives you a cup of water *in my name because you belong to Christ* will certainly not lose his reward (Mark 9:41, italics mine).

The following are three ways to be sure your care is distinctively pastoral.

1. **Just be you.** Because you are a Christian, your presence will emit your unique Christian aroma so don't try to be like someone else.
2. **Be intentional about initiating a sense of the presence of God:**
 - Articulate faith. For example: When problems surface say, "I believe God will help you." Give words of encourage-

ment. And when blessings come, share words such as "I believe God has chosen you for a special blessing."

- Pray *for* and *with* people. Either assure them you will pray for them, or pray with them on the spot. Immediate prayer is the better of the two. We have a lay pastor who, in the process of talking with a person, will ask, "Would you like one of my 30-second prayers?" Then he places his hand upon the person's shoulder and prays. When he does this with me, I really feel pastored.

3. **Accept the stake you have in the spiritual lives of others.**
- Desire their spiritual growth, and do what you can to help them along.
- Grieve over their known weaknesses and sins. Note: Be careful about being judgmental; be pastoral!
- Concern yourself with their church participation.
- Never forget that you are a member of your church's pastoral team, not just someone trying to do good. As an authentic pastor you are concerned for the spiritual lives of those you are called to shepherd.

Now, let's look at the *care* of "pastoral care." Your caring attitude and caring acts demonstrate that you desire the best for your people. Your sense of call, that God is calling you to be His "love with skin on it" to them, creates the right attitude and acts. Your loving and caring spirit will penetrate their inner atmosphere like your cologne penetrates their outer atmosphere.

The visible acts of caring take the forms of "A" and "C" in P A C E.

"A": you are *available* to them in whatever way you can be. This might range from baby-sitting or helping with wallpapering a room to providing transportation. On the other hand, your availability may be referring the person to others rather than doing these things yourself. It may even be saying, "I know what you are facing and though I can't be the one to help you, I can pray for you and be on the lookout for someone who can help."

"C": you *contact* them regularly. This takes the place of what vocational pastors used to do. They called on their people once or twice a year. As good as this was, it was only a token of what was needed.

The pastor usually had his favorites. An older couple told me how Pastor Jones came to their house often. He would make himself at home, pour a cup of coffee and look in the cookie jar. He would swap stories, laugh and cry with them and worry about their children as though they were his own. They were obviously among his favorites.

Pastors do not do this today. That age is past. But God wants each of His people to be treated like His "favorite." Thus lay pastors today give His children special care in a way superior to the old-time visits. Each lay pastor has 5 to 10 "favorite" households. This way *every* household in the church is given special attention.

The lay pastor who is trusted with this ministry must determine the kind of contact he or she has time to make. It may be a personal home visit, phone call, card or letter, invitation to a backyard barbecue, chatting at the grocery store or after the church service. We ask that our lay pastors make two home visit contacts a year.

What kind of person does it take to do pastoral care ministry? The person who *wants* to do it, the one who has the passion for it.

A SENSE OF CALL

One of the members of our National Lay Pastors Advisory Group was deciding whether he should continue on the team. My simple off-the-cuff formula was challenging to him. "There are two issues," I said. "First: Does God want this ministry? Second: Does God want you to be doing it?" These two questions are the bottomline issues for any person who is trying to determine what God wants her or him to do.

Regarding a lay pastoral care ministry in your church, does God want it, and does God want you to be doing it? Let's say that the answer to both questions is *yes*. *This is your call!* I have discovered that of all the missing links between laypeople and ministry, a sense of *call* is the most common.

Why do we use the term *call*? This word is an integral part of the history of the Christian Church. Jesus started it. He *called* to Peter and Andrew while they were casting their nets into the lake, "Come, follow me, and I will make you fishers of men" (Matt. 4:19). Again, He saw Matthew at the tax collector's booth and *called*, "Follow me" (9:9).

The Greek word translated *call* in the New Testament is *kaleo* (pronounced kal-eh'-o), meaning:

- Called or invited by God.
- Called to some office.
- Invited to participate in it and to enjoy it.
- Summoned to do something.

Kaleo is the word used in Matthew 18:2 to tell that Jesus called a little child to Himself, and in Acts 23:17 to tell that Paul summoned the centurion to send him on an errand.

When I was questioned by Presbytery as a candidate for ordination, I was asked, "Why do you believe you are called to be a minister of the gospel?" I had no visible or audible experience to report.

My reply was a quotation I remembered from somewhere, "The heart has reasons that reason does not understand." They accepted this.

Every layperson (volunteer minister) should have as definite a call as every pastor (vocational minister). We clergy have no monopoly on call! Most laypeople erroneously believe we do. God invites every Christian to participate in His work and reveals what that work should be. He would neither cheat any of His people nor assign them to second class by choosing not to call them or failing to make the call known.

Hearing the Call

"How can I hear God's call?" you ask. It's seldom easy, for me anyway. But His Spirit communicates with our spirits, and being quiet in His presence allows that communication to happen.

Many times God speaks to us through others. We need one another. It may be that some hear God best and have the clearest sense of call when they are in a dialogue with brothers and sisters in Christ.

He often speaks to us through our leaders, through hearing about needs and opportunities, through the church newsletter, pulpit announcements or other common means. If we mistake one of these voices for the voice of God, and find ourselves in the wrong ministry, that's okay. We can get out again. By trying something, we may discover what God is *not* calling us to do.

It is every Christian's responsibility to discover what God wants him or her to do. And we should not quit prospecting for this gold until we find it. It's well worth the search.

Seek help if you need it. Many fine spiritual gifts and ministry inventories and programs are available to help you do this. Among the most simple and yet effective is Dr. Kenneth Kinghorn's six-step self-administered test included in my first book.[3] Because so many have been helped by it, I have included it in this book, too:

1. Open yourself to God as a channel for His use.
2. Examine your aspirations for Christ in service.
3. Identify the needs you believe to be most crucial in the life of your church.
4. Evaluate the results of your efforts to serve and to minister.
5. Follow the guidance of the Holy Spirit as He leads you into obedience to Christ.
6. Remain alert to the responses of other Christians.

It may be time to ask, "Where are you regarding your call to ministry?" Let's look at how five people became His disciples. This should alert us to ways He distinctively engages each one of us.

- Andrew was a disciple of John the Baptist. He offered himself to Jesus. Jesus accepted him. His acceptance constituted his call (see John 1:35-39).
- Peter was brought to Jesus by his brother, Andrew. Jesus accepted him also (see vv. 40-42). His acceptance was his call.
- Philip was found by Jesus, who took the initiative in calling him to follow (see v. 43).
- Nathaniel was skeptical. His friend, Philip, was so excited about finding Jesus that he invited Nathaniel to "Come and see." This soon-to-be disciple was sure that nothing good could come out of Nazareth, Jesus' hometown. However, when he met Jesus, he became an instant believer (see vv. 44-46).
- Matthew was called while working. Jesus spotted him at the table collecting taxes and called him. Matthew got up immediately and followed (see Matt. 9:9).

Whether you are already spiritually committed and take the initiative to enlist as did Andrew, or follow another's urging as did Peter, or are sought out by Jesus as was the case with Philip, or approach Him with skepticism as did Nathaniel, or have no previous thought or inclination as did Matthew, know that Jesus is calling you, and He is Lord of the process.

PASTORAL GIFTS

We all have cars. If a car is to get anywhere, the power has to be transferred from the engine to the wheels. The gears—a set of toothed wheels—form the central mechanism to transfer this power. If the gears do not engage one another (or "mesh"), the engine can run at high speed, but the car will not go anywhere.

Christian ministry operates in much the same way. The two gear wheels that have to mesh are *call* and *gifts*. When they mesh, the energy we expend moves our ministries forward, creating results that far exceed our best human efforts. The ministry power released when call and gifts engage is colorfully sketched by the following words:

> God uses what you have to fill a need you never could have filled.
> God uses where you are to take you where you never could have gone.
> God uses what you can do to accomplish what you never could have done.
> God uses who you are to let you become who you never could have been.[4]

I wrote several pages about *call*. Now, what about the other gear wheel, *spiritual gifts*? Paul almost insults us when he confronts us about our knowledge of spiritual gifts: "Now about spiritual gifts, brothers [and sisters], I do not want you to be ignorant" (1 Cor. 12:1).

Is his assumption that we are ignorant of them? This reminds me of what the popular comedian Bill Cosby (Dr. Huxtable on the old Bill Cosby TV show) told his son-in-law. It became clear to him that Alvin did not understand women. "Young man," he said, "You are a smart, intelligent young man, but you are dumb!"

Could Paul be saying to those who do not understand spiritual gifts, "You are a smart, knowledgeable, bright Christian; but you are dumb!"? Many of God's wonderful people admit that they are "dumb" when it comes to spiritual gifts. One Presbyterian elder confided to me at a retreat that she wished she knew what her spiritual gifts were. Many Christians grope for a sense of their spiritual gifts.

Because "spiritual gifts" are *spiritual* their essence is love, joy, peace and other inner qualities (see Gal. 5:22). *Spiritual* also indicates the source—the Spirit of God. Their origin is neither genetic nor environmental; we neither inherit nor learn them. Their distribution is determined by the Giver, not by our choice and not by the Church's practice of assigning, delegating or electing.

Gifts indicate that they are given. They are not earned, merited or planned. They cannot be generated by our wills, produced by our zeal or conferred by church leaders. Gifts differ from skills in that gifts are abilities we are given; they cannot be taught. Skills are abilities we acquire through learning and practice. The two are related in that skills enhance the effectiveness of our spiritual gifts.

Paul spends three chapters educating us about spiritual gifts in 1 Corinthians 12—14. He makes a list of them. Then he tells us that they won't work without love. Next, he gives some counsel about the use and misuse of them. He also writes about spiritual gifts in Romans 12 and Ephesians 4. Peter writes about them in 1 Peter 4. (By the way, *spiritual gifts* can also be called *ministry gifts*, or just *gifts*. One teacher coined the word, *giftabilities*. I like it.) The following grid on the four scriptures show six elements they each have in common:

Scripture	Everyone	Source	List	Use	Love	Benefits
Romans 12:4-9	"Each of us" v. 4	"Grace given" v. 6	seven vs. 6-8	"Use it" v. 6	"Love" v. 9	"The will of God" v. 2
1 Corinthians 12-14	"To each one" 12:7	"The Spirit" 12:7-11	thirteen 12:7-10, 28	"Given for" 12:7	"Love" 13:1-13	"Build up the church" 14:12
1 Peter 4:8-11	"Each one" v. 10	"God's grace" v. 10	three vs. 9, 11	"Do it" v. 11	"Love" v. 8	Others served v. 10
Ephesians 4:7, 8, 11-13	"To each one" v. 7	"Christ" v. 7	five v. 11	"Prepare God's people" v. 12	"Love" v. 2	Body of Christ Built up v. 12

Three simple sentences tell it all:

- God gives gifts for ministry.
- God gives gifts to every Christian.
- God expects His gifts to be used with love.

Three of the 27 spiritual gifts listed in the New Testament make up a cluster of gifts for pastoral care: *mercy, encouragement* and *service*. If a person has any one of the three, he or she will be able to be a lay pastor.

Mercy is an inner awareness or feeling of compassion for others; wanting to bring help; being sympathetic or empathic; the feelings and/or thoughts ignited by another's life situation.

Encouragement is to come alongside of another to comfort, console, embolden, inspire, reassure, cheer, give courage. It includes a touch of admonition, confrontation and exhortation for the purpose of strengthening or helping.

Service is attending as a servant, to aid or relieve another, to offer care, to express Christian affection in practical ways, bestowing comfort and help.

If, while reading the descriptions of the pastoral gift cluster, you ,aid to yourself, *That's me!* your next thought must be, *I can do this!* You *can* do it!

The sure way to discover your gifts is to begin doing a ministry for which you think you may have the *call* and *gift*. Be alert to how the gear wheels within you engage each other. If you sense the gears grinding rather than meshing, you may want to consider and pray about changing to another ministry.

One of our lay pastors opted out of the Lay Pastors Ministry to devote himself to the music and worship ministry in our church. That's okay. Why grind the gears? Someone from the music and worship ministry whose gears are grinding in that ministry may give himself or herself to the Lay Pastors Ministry.

If a person is not doing ministry it is likely to be for one of three reasons: (1) the gears—call and gifts—have not yet engaged; or (2) they are "stripped"—call and gift do not match; or (3) overuse—burnout. The kind of person who can do pastoral care ministry is one who is *called* and *gifted*.

chapter ten

ASKING TO BE EQUIPPED

A former colleague of mine, a genius in creating acronyms, maintained that we need FAT people for ministry:

- Faithful
- Available
- Teachable

Faithful and available speak for themselves. Teachable means a person is open to being equipped. Ephesians 4:11,12, "[to equip] the saints for the work of ministry" (*NKJV*) makes equipping an indispensable part of God's formula for ministry.

> "My job is to make men do what they don't want to do so they can become what they want to be."
> —Vince Lombardi

We don't rush into ministry with only enthusiasm and faith. The Greek word is *katartismos*, which has a cluster of meanings that compel us to be prepared for doing God's work. This cluster includes:

- To be perfected;
- To put in order, adjust;
- To be trained, instructed;
- To make one be what he or she is created to be;
- To outfit with necessities;
- To completely furnish.

The equipping *program* may take only a few hours; the *process* continues throughout life. For example, the equipping *program* at our church gives lay pastors between 10 and 15 hours of training. The *program* is soon over. The *process* goes on while they do their ministries.

Equipping must not be taken lightly. I have known some churches that treated it as optional, allowing people to become lay pastors without any equipping, and other churches that lowered their standards. This makes for a weak ministry and often a failed ministry.

It is God who calls Christians to care for His people and to be equipped! Therefore, we must do it, do it well, and require it of all who do ministry. Equipping calls for discipline on the part of leaders. Vince Lombardi, the legendary coach of the Green Bay Packers, was asked by a person seated next to him on a plane, "What is your job?"

His reply: "My job is to make men do what they don't want to do so they can become what they want to be." Lay pastors want to be successful ministers, so we dare not shortchange them either by not requiring equipping or by doing it poorly.

Equipping is so important that vocational ministers are required to get basic (or seminary) training, followed with "continuing education" annually. Most churches write this into their terms of *call* with a budget item to make it possible. Though the amount of equipping is not the same for volunteer ministers, being equipped is just as important, and the church is just as obligated to provide and require both the program and the process.

"Those who have ears, let them hear what the Spirit is saying to the churches": pastors and teachers are to equip the saints for the work of ministry.

READY TO OBEY AND SERVE

At one of my seminars in Pennsylvania, a man stood to his feet and exclaimed, "Sir, in the Church of Jesus Christ there are no volunteers! We are either obedient to God or disobedient!" He said this with conviction. He is right.

Moses, when called by God, had five good reasons *not* to do what God was calling him to do. He was attracted by the bush which, though burning, was not consumed. God used that phenomenon to get his attention so he could call him to go to Egypt and liberate his people. God has his ways of getting our attention, doesn't He!

The account of Moses is given in chapters 3 and 4 of Exodus. (The following is my paraphrase of the account.)

God said, "I have come down to rescue my people from slavery." Moses was thrilled to hear this, but his thrill was short-lived. It turned into a chill when God told him how he was going to do it: "I am sending you."

Moses pulled back. He resisted God on five fronts: identity, authority, acceptance, competence and volition. Do these sound strangely familiar? I have resisted God on all these fronts, and unless you are very different, you have too.

The word "but" must have alerted God to Moses' strong objections. Moses' response should have been, "Okay God, what do I do first?" But who can fault him? The task was huge.

The first resistance:

"Who am I that I should do this?" He felt unworthy and unprepared. Not bad reasoning. He *was* unworthy and unprepared for such a task. But that was not the issue. The issue was that God called him to do it. It was an *identity* issue. The question, "Who am I?" (3:11) is not the right one. The right one is, Who is calling me? Moses missed the fact that God has the right to call anyone He chooses. Moses was God's servant. God, being understanding and patient, promised, "I will be with you" (v. 12).

The second resistance:

"I don't have the authority. They will ask, 'Who sent you?'" Of course, he didn't have the authority in and of himself. No one had commissioned him—until now. The issue was one of *authority*. God gave him authority on the spot: "Tell them I AM [Jehovah] has sent me to you."

The third resistance:

"What if they do not accept me?" This issue was one of *acceptance*. No one wants to enter a situation where rejection is a risk. The likelihood of being rejected was real. But so what? A lost battle doesn't mean a lost war. God gave Moses two signs to assure eventual acceptance.

The fourth resistance:

"I am not competent." This was no flimsy excuse; he was not competent. On the issue of *competence*, you and I need Paul's admission followed by his assurance to the Corinthian Christians, "Not that we are competent in ourselves...our competence comes from God. He has made us competent as ministers" (2 Cor. 3:5,6). God's promise, "Now go; I will help you speak and will teach you what to say," should have brought him to obedience.

The fifth resistance:
"Oh, Lord (he still called him Lord), please send someone else to do it." The issue now was *volition*. He didn't want to go. This angered God. Then we read, "Moses went."

God's anger did it! Moses must have still felt uncertain, but he knew God meant business. By being obedient throughout the ensuing months, Moses discovered how much God meant business. The Lord *was* with him. Moses *did* have authority—his people and the pharaoh took him seriously. He *was* accepted, he *was* competent—he got the job done.

All of Moses' objections are very real for people called to be lay pastors. Who is worthy to pastor others? Who has authority to be a pastor? Who does not fear rejection? Who is competent to do God's work? Who would not prefer someone else doing the really hard tasks? Our objections can seem valid, because they are born of the first part of these two-part truths:

- You are not worthy; however, God's call makes you worthy.
- You do not have the authority; however, God gives you authority.
- You may not be accepted; however, God will use you anyway.
- You are not competent; however, God is your competence.
- You want someone else to go; however, God has chosen you.

I do not believe God minds hearing our objections. He has been listening to peoples' objections for millennia. In fact, whatever our true thoughts and feelings, we need to get them out. God will not chasten or shame us. He will listen carefully, then graciously assure us of His presence and provisions. He just wants us to hang in there until all the reasons are out. Then we are ready to obey with our whole hearts.

Returning to the words of the man who said, "In the Church, there are no volunteers. We are either obedient to God or disobedient" and remembering that every Christian is a minister, let's look at the difference between a volunteer and a minister:

A *volunteer* offers himself or herself for service;
A *minister* responds to a call from God for service.

A *volunteer's* service is an option at his or her convenience;
A *minister's* service is not an option, but is a matter of obedience to God.

> # Obey and serve are two sides of the same coin. Obedience is the inner attitude. Serving is the outer act.

A *volunteer* is master of his or her own life and time;
A *minister* acknowledges Jesus as Lord of his or her life and time.

A *volunteer* is accountable to the organization and its leaders;
A *minister* is accountable first to God, then to the organization and its leaders.

A *volunteer* is motivated by need and recognition;
A *minister* is motivated by the Spirit, the Christian community and need.

A *volunteer* reserves the right to choose what he or she will do;
A *minister* relinquishes the choice of what he or she will do to the higher principle of spiritual gifts and divine call.

So...the man was right. We are not volunteers; we are obedient servants. And by being obedient, we experience what Jesus meant by, "Whoever wants to save his life will lose it, but whoever loses his life for me will find it" (Matt. 16:25). Losing one's life equates with obedience to God's call.

Obey and serve are two sides of the same coin. Obedience is the inner attitude. Serving is the outer act.

READY TO GROW SPIRITUALLY

A comic who conducts humor workshops across the country quipped, "I once heard the expression, 'Smooth runs the water when the brook is deep.' I'm deep, but down deep, I'm shallow." This might not be as much quip as truth. One who is to do ministry must be committed to deepening his or her spiritual life. Don Postema, in *Space For God*, says it best:

> The world really doesn't need more "busy people," maybe not even more intelligent people. It needs deep people, people who know that they need: solitude, if they are going to find out who they are; silence, if their words are to mean anything; reflection, if their actions are to have any significance; contemplation, if they are to see the world as it really is; prayer, if they are going to be conscious of God, if they are to "know God and enjoy God forever."[5]

My time with God: reading the Bible; sitting back to reflect upon it (sometimes making notes, writing in the margins or underlining with green, red and black ink) and praying...does four things for me:

1. It helps me *believe*.
2. It helps my *discipleship*.
3. It helps my *identity* as a servant of God.
4. It helps in my *relationship* with God.

Reading the Bible, meditation and prayer have been known as "disciplines" throughout the centuries because discipline is required to persevere. The kind of person it takes for this ministry is one who is committed to disciplined spiritual growth.

If you are a lay pastor, your time with God will impact your people in ways you may not even notice. (Let's call them "your people" because God gave them to you to care for.) Moses is a prime example of this.

After spending 40 days and 40 nights with God on the mountain, the record in Exodus 34 reports: "When Moses came down from Mount Sinai with the two tablets of the Testimony in his hands, he was not aware that his face was radiant because he had spoken with the Lord" (v. 29).

When you connect with your people, they will know you have been with the Lord. How? They just will. There is a mystery about this. This must be what 2 Corinthians 3:18 means:

> And we, who with unveiled faces all reflect the Lord's glory, are being transformed into his likeness with an ever-increasing glory, which comes from the Lord, who is the Spirit.

Evidence of being with the Lord was seen again on the Day of Pentecost. The 120 believers came together to pray, wait and worship. The Holy Spirit descended upon them. Their behavior was changed. What happened to them dismayed the unbelievers so much that some thought they were drunk. Because these Christians were so unaware of what the Spirit was doing in them, they even asked each other, "What does this mean?" (Acts 2:12).

Later, two of the apostles unknowingly amazed the rulers, elders, teachers of the law and priests with another form of the same phenomenon:

> When they saw the courage of Peter and John and realized that they were unschooled, ordinary men, they were astonished and *they took note that these men had been with Jesus* (Acts 4:13, italics mine).

Moses' face was radiant; the apostles spoke in other tongues; Peter and John astonished the religious leaders with their charisma—all because they spent time with God. If you will covenant with God to spend quality time with Him each day, you will favorably influence your people in ways far beyond what you could plan. Your part in pastoral care is to spend time with God and with your people. His part is to make your caring initiatives effective. It will happen!

The following story illustrates what you have just read. A prominent Bible teacher was invited by a church to give a series of lectures. At each gathering, he noticed a delightful, flowerlike fragrance permeating the room. After the second evening, he asked the pastor where that delightful aroma came from. The pastor explained that a few people who worked at the perfume factory had to come directly from their work to the meetings. Unknown to them, their clothes, having absorbed the fragrance of their environment, were releasing it into the room.

We may not be aware of absorbing God's "aroma" when we are with Him and releasing it when we are with people, but we do; and because we do, our ministry is effective. Knowledge and skills are useful tools, but they alone will not do the job of caring for God's people in the way He wants. This principle was championed way back in the 1920s by Evelyn Underhill, a lay woman who gave a series of talks to Anglican priests in England:

> Attention to God must be your primary religious activity, and this for the strictly practical reason that without that attention to God, all other religious activities will lose their worth....Other things, intellectual and social aptitudes, good preaching, a capacity for organization...help this work and help it much. None of these, however, is essential. Prayer is!

READY FOR "WHATEVER"

The delights, joys and fulfillment while doing ministry are far greater than one anticipates when starting. However, pain is also a part of ministry. Jesus promised that our joy would be full, and He assured us that we would find "life" in doing ministry. But He also talked about taking up our cross. Christian ministry is both pleasurable and painful. One who is to be a lay pastor has to be ready for both.

Paul experienced the pain of caring: "My dear children, for whom I am again in the pains of childbirth until Christ is formed in you" (Gal. 4:19). But his pain was more than offset by joy, for the Christians in the church at Philippi were his "joy and crown" (Phil. 4:1). Jesus also knew both joy and pain in ministry. So will lay pastors. They have to be ready for "whatever." They have to be willing to be "at risk," to venture beyond security, convenience and comfort.

Somewhere I read, "If you have no anxiety, the risk you face is probably not worthy of you. If you create a life that is always comfortable, always without risk, you have created a fool's paradise."

Rejection
Three sources of pain are common for those who care for others. The

first is *rejection*. A compassionate, loving person will always risk pain because of the possibility of not being accepted. Being rejected hurts! As we saw earlier, one of Moses' chief reasons for resisting God's call was, "What if they do not believe me or listen to me?" (Exod. 4:1). Most lay pastors fear this and in some cases the fear is warranted.

But you are in good company. Jesus is the ultimate sufferer of rejection: "He came to that which was his own, *but his own did not receive him*" (John 1:11, italics mine). The pain of rejection is the cost of doing business. The business in our case is caring for God's people. Nonacceptance, or even a cool rejection, really penetrates tenderhearted, sensitive, self-giving and loving people. It hurts!

Trauma

The second cause of pain is *trauma*. I recall one lay pastor who was assigned a person who happened to be in the hospital at the time. What an opportunity to get acquainted. As she walked down the hall to make her visit, she heard over the intercom, "Code Blue! Code Blue!" Nurses and doctors were pouring into the room where she was going. This was the first time in her life she had seen a person die. She experienced trauma, emotional shock. She hurt! And she continued hurting for some time.

This, of course, is quite an uncommon occurrence. But lesser traumatizing experiences are also painful. Accidents, terminal illnesses, miscarriages, amputations, divorces, financial collapses and other such unnerving tragedies cause pain. When you become a lay pastor, you open yourself to the risk of pain inflicted by traumatic events.

Failure

The third is *failure*. You will occasionally make mistakes and, because of them, feel you have failed. This hurts to the quick. It is humiliating. But wait! All is not lost. Failure in its various forms of mistakes, incompetence, stupidity, misunderstanding and delinquency can be positive. Some failures are only perceived failures and therefore not really failures at all. Other failures are true failures (even disasters), but these are excellent teachers. By learning from our failures, we convert them into successes.

Jesus, our best model for ministry, never failed; but His disciples, also excellent models, did fail in many ways and on many occasions:

1. They could not help a boy in his affliction. His father was in despair. This form of failure is *incompetence*.
2. They didn't see how they could possibly feed 5,000 famished people. This form of failure is *error in judgment* and *ignorance* of what Jesus could do.
3. They didn't hear Jesus well because they argued about who would be the greatest. This form of failure is *pride* and *jealousy*. They lapsed into their pre-disciple lives.
4. They really missed it when they turned away the parents of little children. This form of failure was their *authoritarian* and *officious spirit*.
5. They became angry with the Samaritans who would not accept them. They wanted to destroy them with fire from heaven, calling down the wrath of God. This form of failure was *vindictiveness*.
6. They slept while Jesus agonized in prayer. This form of failure might have been only *physical weakness*, but more than likely they *lacked empathy* and did not read the seriousness of Jesus' struggle.
7. Peter struck out with a sword, wounding one of those who had come to take Jesus captive. This form of failure was *over-defensiveness* in a threatening circumstance.
8. They went back to fishing after Jesus' crucifixion. This form of failure was *loss of vision* and probably *self-pity*.
9. After Jesus' resurrection and even after Pentecost when he had the advantage of the Holy Spirit's presence, Peter continued to discriminate against non-Jews. This form of failure was *lack of understanding* for the width of God's love, the extensiveness of Jesus' sacrifice and the inclusiveness of the Church.

What a bunch of failures, these disciples! One of Peter's failures caused him such great pain that he went outside and wept bitterly. Failure hurts! It can demoralize a lay pastor and ruin his or her ministry. The disciples obviously recovered from their failures, learned from them, put them behind and moved on to found the Church and fulfill the Great Commission.

So there we have it, a profile of the kind of person it takes to be a lay pastor. One who...

- Thinks "direction," not perfection;
- Wants to do the ministry;
- Has a sense of call;
- Has the pastoral gifts;
- Asks to be equipped;
- Is ready to obey and serve;
- Is growing spiritually;
- Is ready for "whatever."

Please don't wait for these qualities to ripen in your life before you begin ministering. If you do, you will be like the couple pictured in a cartoon who waited until they could afford to get married. The groom with the aid of a cane was pushing the bride down the aisle in a wheelchair.

Seriously consider the first paragraph of this chapter. It shows that you probably have what it takes right now to be a lay pastor. You will grow in maturity as you minister, just as the disciples did, and just as every Christian since then has done.

If you are mature enough to have read this far in a book about lay ministry, you cannot use, "I'm not ready yet," as an excuse not to be equipped for ministry. The issue is not ability; it is obedience. Commit yourself and go for it!

"He who has an ear, let him hear what the Spirit says to the churches." People, if pastoring is your call, then for God's sake, do it!

Note: For a Lab, see appendix D.

Notes:
1. Bruce L. Bugbee, *Networking*, (1989): 4, 106-108.
2. Melvin J. Steinbron, *Can the Pastor Do It Alone?* (Ventura, Calif.: Regal Books, 1987) p. 63-66.
3. Ibid., p. 68.
4. Tim Hansel, *Holy Sweat* (Waco, Tex.: Word Books, 1987) p. 25.
5. Quoted by Rowland Croucher, *Rivers in the Desert* (Sutherland NSW, Australia, Albatross Books, 1991) p. 58.

Why Laypeople Can Pastor

WHO IS THE PASTOR?

Who is Brian's pastor? Is it the ordained pastor or the lay pastor?

Brian is "mentally challenged." Hope Church had a large pastoral staff, but no one was giving Brian pastoral care on a regular basis.

I did not fault them; there could not have been a more committed and competent staff anywhere. They were doing all the caring they could do. It was not humanly possible, however, for any vocational pastor or group of pastors to give the kind of continuing care Brian needed and deserved as a member of God's family.

Al Taylor became a lay pastor four years ago, and Brian became one of his charges. Al began to contact him almost weekly, and continues to attend his swimming meets, pray for him, read the Bible with him, connect with his parents and occasionally take him to lunch. Brian's and Al's lives have bonded. Brian is happy. His parents are relieved. Al is fulfilled. Again the question: Who is Brian's pastor? Al Taylor, to be sure.

Who is Scott and Kathy Cartwright's pastor?

They were devastated when Kathy gave birth to a child with Down's syndrome. Ruth Connors, who had just become a lay pastor, took them into her flock. She also took them into her heart. Early in the relationship Ruth wrote an encouraging letter which, in reading between the lines, assured both Scott and Kathy that she understood their plight. Ruth had been there. She visited them, sat with and for them as needed and kept in touch by phone.

An amazing level of understanding was evident. Scott and Kathy knew she knew. Their testimony is that Ruth comforted them with the comfort she had received from the Lord (see 2 Cor. 1:4). Ruth had requested that they be in her pastoring group. Her availability at the time of their need indicates that the timing was of God.

A member of the pastoral staff was also of special help at this time, being at the hospital often and ministering in other ways. Another pastoral staff person gave Scott and Kathy needed support through visits and prayer. Those two pastors and Ruth made an ideal pastoral team, each giving their unique form of loving care. The result was well-rounded pastoral care.

As you would expect, the staff members needed to give attention to the steady procession of other critical needs, but Ruth continues her supportive and helpful caring. She provides an unbroken flow of love and care through the days and weeks. It is clear that she is the continuing pastor of all four Cartwrights (their family also includes a lively three-year-old daughter).[1]

I hear similar stories often. In my position as founder of the Lay Pastors Ministry and president of Lay Pastors Ministry, Inc., I talk on the phone with ministry leaders from all across the United States, Canada, the Bahamas, Australia and South Africa. I also read many of their newsletters, conduct training and information seminars and have the privilege of visiting with those who stop by. It is moving to hear what they are telling me.

Let's visit one of the churches in our network, Saint John's Evangelical Lutheran Church in Statesville, North Carolina. This congregation started its Lay Pastors Ministry in 1991. The ministry includes 337 families. (Within my acquaintance, churches having the Lay Pastors Ministry range in size from 35 to 7,000 members.)

Saint John's lay ministers (as they call their lay pastors) made 2,717 contacts in 1996. One of their members prepares a computer-generated graph periodically that shows not only the number of contacts, but also the kind of contacts.[2]

In a typical month, February 1996, its lay ministers made a total of 17 home visits, 110 other face-to-face visits, 107 telephone calls and mailed 64 cards or letters and connected in 26 other ways. This adds up to 324 quality contacts in one month, 2,717 in one year. The graph cannot show the daily prayers for the people, the perpetual availability for times of need or the mutual bonding of lives by the cumulative value of continuing contacts. By the way, they post the graph on the lay ministry bulletin board for the entire congregation to see.

Imagine what the effect of this ministry will be when they have enough lay ministers to include all the households of this congregation. How many significant contacts could one or two vocational pastors make in a year? How many people could they meaningfully and daily pray for? How many people could they get close to and know as well as the lay ministers know them?

And the Lay Pastors Ministry is just one lay pastoral care model among many being used by churches today. Others are the Stephen Ministries, BeFriender Ministry, People's Ministries and more.[3] Each has its unique approach; the common denominator is equipping the laity to pastorally care for God's people.

Do pastors of churches who give the congregational care to qualified laity not care about their people? Just the opposite. They care for the people so much that they shepherd the system that makes every-member care possible. Like Moses, they give their immediate attention to the leaders, turning the day-by-day, person-to-person pastoral care over to qualified people.

Vocational pastors and volunteer pastors are truly "partners in ministry," literally "copastors." The vocational pastor is the generalist, caring for the larger matters: preaching, teaching, counseling, crises intervention, marrying and burying. The volunteer pastor is the specialist, giving grassroots, customized care to a manageable number of households. Vocational pastors are informed about the large things happening in people's lives, but they have no way of knowing the difficulty Joe is having at work, the Smith's pain caused by their prodigal son, the stress in the Peterson's marriage or Linda's anxiety about her upcoming outpatient surgery.

Nor does the vocational pastor know about new cars, new recipes, new landscaping, individual graduations, vacation trips, beginning pregnancies, birthdays, anniversaries and other celebrative events. While the volunteer pastor is praying for each of his, her or their people (some are husband-wife caring teams), the vocational pastor is praying for issues such as next Sunday's sermon, the board meeting, the leaders of the lay ministries and the plans to enlarge the sanctuary.

The basic task of the vocational pastor is not to pastor the individual members, but to pastor the church. If the pastor will give spiritual leadership to the church, lay ministries will flourish. But pastors can't do this effectively if their energies are given to person-to-person pastoral care.

Stevens and Collins write: "This gives the pastor a new job description. 'I see the pastor,' Mansell Pattison says, 'as essentially a shepherd of systems. The pastor functions to nurture and guide the subsystems of the church.' Pastoral care is 'care of the living systems,' not just the care of individual saints."[4]

The following descriptions designate the kind of caring attention given by volunteer lay pastors (the specialists) compared to that given by vocational pastors (the generalists):

Volunteer Pastors	Vocational Pastors
Grassroots care	Overall care
One-on-one care	Care of all members
Basic congregational care	Nurture, mobilize, equip
Ongoing pastoral care	Emergency, short-term care
"One anothering" (1 Thess. 5:11)	Care of the whole church
Regular care	Crisis and special needs care
Care on a continuing basis	Seriate care
Hands-on care	The larger matters
Frontline care	General care

The three reasons laypeople can be the frontline pastors of the congregation are:

1. God gives the ministry to them;
2. Their church gives the ministry to them;
3. They have the passion and the skills.

God Gives the Ministry to Them

God gives the ministry to ordinary people. Along with the assignment, He gives the power to succeed. We tend to attribute a larger-than-life stature to people to whom God gives ministry. We think of the patriarchs, prophets and kings of the Old Testament: people such as Abraham, Moses and David. We think of the apostles of the New Testament: people such as Peter, John and Paul. We think of church figures throughout history, people such as Augustine, Luther, Wesley, Mother Teresa and Billy Graham.

A close look, however, reveals that God gives ministry mostly to ordinary people. Gideon, to whom God gave the task of liberating Israel from the oppressive control of Midian, was the least in his family and his family was the weakest clan in the tribe of Manasseh. A very ordinary man indeed; unknown, unlikely, untrained and inexperienced. This is how he saw himself and this is how he was (see Judges 6—8).

But God saw Gideon as a "mighty man of valor" (6:12, *RSV*). The record tells us that "the Spirit of the Lord came upon Gideon" (v. 34). His success was not in his outstanding ability, but in his obedience to God's call.

Amos was an ordinary shepherd when God called him to be a prophet to the northern cities of Israel. His effectiveness was not in his great insights and oratory, but in God's call (see Amos 1:1-11). By listening to God, he was able to proclaim, "This is what the Lord says" (v. 11).

We have already seen the unlikeliness of the apostles to whom Jesus committed the building of His church. Their success, which continues in our era and will continue until "The Coming," cannot be credited to their expertise and natural resourcefulness, but to the power of the Spirit that came upon them (see Acts 1:8).

These people are like most of God's ministers, just ordinary people. The same God who gave ministry to them is giving the pastoral care ministry to members of our churches. The same resources God made available to them are available to you and me.

Both Robert Slocum and I believe in ordinary people. He wrote: "I am convinced the effective church for the twenty-first century will be the church that mobilizes, equips, empowers and supports *ordinary* Christians in ministry."

And Slocum defines *ordinary Christians*: "By *ordinary Christians*, I mean the laity, the lay men and women who are not church professionals, yet who make up more than 98 percent of the people of God." He continues, "It is of critical importance for us *ordinary Christians* to understand who we are, what we are supposed to do and where we are supposed to do it."[5]

The foundational Scripture for lay ministry, which I have cited often, Ephesians 4:11,12, makes the point clear: It is God's [ordinary] people who are to be equipped to do the ministry.

There we have it. Laypeople can pastor because God has given the ministry to them. "He who has an ear, let him hear what the Spirit says to the churches." *Let laypeople do it!*

Their Church Gives the Ministry to Them

The church is not acting on its own authority when it gives the ministry of pastoral care to the people. It is only carrying out God's plan.

> "We are not as smart as the laity think we are; and they are not as dumb as we think they are."
> —John Wesley

God gives ministry to all Christians, but the Church *also* must give ministry to its people if lay ministry is to happen.

The church where I serve on the pastoral staff as a part-time member is giving the ministry to the people. The rationale in the Session (official board) Structure Overview is:

> In our commitment to "prepare God's people for works of service" (Eph. 4:11,12), one of the spiritual duties of an elder is to recognize and affirm spiritual gifts for ministry in members of the Body. Mobilizing and training for ministry and mission is a central goal. We need to give permission rather than restrain because the job of Session is to inspire people to take risks for the kingdom of God in new and existing ministries.

The Church has awakened. Both clergy and laity are redrawing what has traditionally been a very small circle of ministers, making it large enough to include all Christians. Some churches are finally "letting" laypeople do it. History records many attempts at this. Martin

Luther had the "priesthood of believers" theology, but lacked the strategy to implement it as far as ministry was concerned.

John Wesley trained 653 laypeople to preach and pastor in the eighteenth century. He was severely criticized for doing this by other Anglican clergy. His response to them was, "We are not as smart as the laity think we are; and they are not as dumb as we think they are."⁶

> Only pastors who genuinely believe
> that laypeople are as authentically
> called as they themselves are can give
> the kind of support laypeople need.

Support from the pastor is an integral part of the church giving the ministry to the people. Only pastors who genuinely believe that laypeople are as authentically called as they themselves are can give the kind of support laypeople need. Any tongue-in-cheek acceptance of lay ministry will covertly signal lack of support.

On the other hand, once pastors have been freed from any doubt that laypeople are equally called by God, their conviction and confidence will covertly signal support. Pastors can give support by affirming and celebrating lay ministry, commending lay pastors from the pulpit, giving them opportunities to tell about their ministries in worship services and being available to personally counsel and encourage them.

Commissioning laypeople during a worship service by the laying on of hands announces to the members that the church is giving the pastoral care ministry to their peers. It prepares the members to receive from lay pastors. It also confirms in the minds of the lay pastors that the ministry is theirs, that they are authentic members of the pastoral team.

Lay pastors are bona fide pastors because of what I call their "ministryfolio." Whereas a "portfolio" is the office and function of a minister of state, a "ministryfolio" is the office and function of a minister of Christ. The concept comes from Matthew 10, the record of Jesus giving the ministry to His disciples, sending them out on their own:

- Called (v. 1): Lay pastors are called to pastor people.
- Authority (v. 1): Lay pastors are authorized to pastor people.
- Sent (v. 5): Lay pastors are commissioned to a specific ministry.
- Relationship (v. 6): Lay pastors are to build relationships.
- Competence (vv. 19,20): Lay pastors' competence is from God.
- Courage (v. 26): Lay pastors do not fear rejection.
- Sacrifice (v. 38): Lay pastors bear whatever crosses they must.
- Obedience (v. 38): Lay pastors are servants.
- Incarnational Principle (v. 40): Christ is in lay pastors.
- Reward (v. 42): Lay pastors shall receive a reward.
- Equipping (11:1): Lay pastors shall be instructed.
- Accountable (Luke 9:10): Lay pastors will be asked to report.

They Have the Passion and the Skills

This is the third reason laypeople can pastor. In 1978 when I saw the first laypeople in Cincinnati begin to make their pastoral visits, I was surprised by their delight. They exuded unexpected passion for what they were doing. They looked forward to their next contacts and the developing relationships. They had found a new joy in their Christian lives. One-on-one pastoral care had always been one of the most fulfilling parts of my total ministry and now I saw laypeople as passionate about it as I.

This was ministry! Their ministry! The ministry for which God had given them gifts, to which He had called them, for which they had been equipped and commissioned!

I can imagine some vocational pastors reading about these excited people and saying, "They can have it." The reason is that many professional pastors do not have pastoral gifts. God did not wire them with mercy, empathy, patience and encouragement. He gave them other gifts: preaching, teaching, administration or evangelism. No one has all the gifts, not even credentialed ministers.

I can imagine many laypeople reading about these excited people and saying, "Let them do it. That's not for me." The people saying this have gifts for other ministries. It goes without saying that no one would have the time or energy to use all the gifts even if he or she had them.

But because of their passion, they can give to people the most valuable thing they have—themselves. Overlooking this, lay pastors will often unnecessarily think they are responsible for changing people. But as my friend, Ken Haugk, founder and executive director of The Stephen Ministries proposes, "Christians are responsible for care; God is responsible for cure."[7] We plant and water, God gives the increase (see 1 Cor. 3:6,7). Giving themselves to others is pastoral care.

This is what Irving Berlin did with music. He only had what he was by nature because he never had formal training. He never learned to read or write music and his piano playing was confined to the key of F sharp. He just gave what he had and what he was—himself. More than 1,000 songs came from giving himself, two of which are *God Bless America* and *White Christmas*. Laypeople can pastor because they can give themselves to their people, a small segment of the total congregation. What Irving Berlin did with music, laypeople can do with pastoring.

In addition to passion, lay pastors have skills. Just as vocational pastors, volunteer pastors possess both natural and acquired skills. And according to my years of seeing them in action, many laypeople are better at pastoring than professionals. In fact, this professional pastor has seen laypeople outstrip him in their ability to accept people, stick with people, empathize with people and build authentic and lasting relationships. They P A C E people more effectively.

Hear and Remember

Laypeople can *hear* and *remember*. These are the two activities that constitute pastoral care. When I recently read this simple definition of pastoral care in John Patton's book *Pastoral Care in Context*,[8] I paused, lifted my eyes from the page and said out loud, "That's it! That's what pastoral care is: *hearing* and *remembering*." Together, they are the essence of P A C E.

When people are *heard*, they know that someone finally understands them and truly knows what they are going through. They "feel" pastored; somebody really cares. When they are *remembered*—greeted on their birthdays, visited or phoned on the anniversaries of their spouses', children's or parents' deaths, prayed with about their illnesses or upcoming surgeries or underachieving children—they know someone truly cares. They are not alone. They have not been forgotten. They "feel" pastored.

Laypeople can do this. They can hear and they can remember because they know what it means to be heard and remembered, or not heard and not remembered. Of course, it helps to have a course in listening skills and a workshop on the significant occasions for connecting with people, but that will come in time. Have you heard, "Anything worth doing is worth doing poorly...until you can do it better" or, "You don't have to know everything before you can do anything"?

Counsel

Laypeople can pastor because they can counsel. Counsel? They can counsel because they can listen, and listening is the key to all counseling...lay or professional. Let me illustrate:

Two Saint Paul, Minnesota police officers were killed by a gunman in August, 1994. The widow of another officer killed five years earlier, who was active in the national organization of such widows, said on a special TV program the day of the funerals with a touch of anger in her voice, "We don't need advice; *we just need someone who will listen to us!*"

Lay pastors can do what the widow asked for: listen and refrain from giving advice. The following is an example of lay counseling:

Dolly Parton, country music star and actress, was asked on the "Donahue" show if she had psychological counseling during her chronic depression, a very painful time in her life. In an uncharacteristically firm voice, I heard her say she did not. She proceeded to tell about her loving and supportive family and friends who helped her get through it. She said "They *counseled* me in a way that God and I were able to work it through."

For decades the Billy Graham crusades have used the designation *counselor* to identify the laypeople who guide seekers to personal faith in Jesus Christ.

It is difficult to use the word *counselor* in referring to a lay pastor because our society is conditioned to think that only credentialed, professional counselors can be effective in helping people who are struggling.

It's time to rescue the word *counseling* from exclusive use by professionals. Two psychologists help with the rescue: Andrew Christiansen, Ph.D., professor of psychology at UCLA, and Neil Jacobson, Ph.D., professor of psychology at the University of Washington. They conclude: "The outcome of therapy is not enhanced by training, education or years of experience. It may not even matter whether there is a live therapist present!"

Virginia Rutter reported the surprising stance of these two psychologists in the March/April 1994 issue of *Psychology Today* in an article titled, "Oops! A Very Embarrassing Story." She continues: "Christiansen and Jacobson contend that no one has made much of an effort to look at therapy delivered by nonprofessionals, despite the fact that it proves just as effective, or more effective, than therapy performed by psychiatrists, psychologists, social workers and family therapists."

She then quotes Dr. Christiansen: "In psychotherapy, it is not clear that the skills of the therapist are any more helpful than the skills of people with life experience in dealing with a problem."

Lay pastors have the "life experience in dealing with a problem." And the potency of "life experience" is heightened by the gifts from the Spirit, the power of the Spirit and the lay pastor's passion to love, hear, remember and care. My belief that lay pastors can counsel is grounded in Scripture:

> Personally I am satisfied...that you yourselves are rich in goodness, amply filled with all [spiritual] knowledge and competent to admonish and *counsel* and instruct one another also (Rom. 15:14, *Amp.*, italics mine).

I believe that lay pastors, being in a Christian environment, have two advantages over professional therapists. First, they can reach out to people in need and continue to pursue them in spite of avoidance, while therapists must wait for clients to initiate the contacts. Our model is the shepherd in Jesus' parable who went out to search for the one lost sheep.

Second, lay pastors learn from Scripture that they are called to influence the lives of people with Christian values and morals.

The "E" of P A C E—Example—is operative in the relationship.

Professionals, on the other hand, being in a secular environment, are required to be value-free and morally neutral.

Lay counseling is not therapy; that is left to the professionals. Nevertheless, lay counseling is therapeutic.

People ask if lay pastors risk litigation for themselves and/or the church. Life is a risk; ministry is a risk. The best counsel I receive is that the chances are minuscule. When the question came up at our last Lay Pastoral Care International Conference, an attorney recommended checking locally for laws, and said that court actions vary from state to state.

Because we live in a litigious culture,[9] four wise actions can be taken to reduce the already long odds of legal action:

1. Do not refer to yourself as a counselor at any time.
2. Avoid using the words "counsel" and/or "counseling."
3. Never permit impropriety in physical contact or closeness.
4. Respect confidentiality; keep private matters private.
5. Ask to be equipped to know when and how to refer a person to a professional.

Laypeople can pastor because they can *counsel*. They don't have to use the term, but they need to know that they can do it.

What's in a Name?

Is the name *lay pastor* appropriate? Many raise this question. In many minds it is an oxymoron. One of our lay pastors explained to me, "I don't think of myself as a pastor; I think of myself as a friend." By renaming herself, she redefined her ministry role. *Pastor* was above and beyond what she perceived herself to be. Friendship has rich value (Jesus called His disciples friends, John 15:15), but friendship is only one part of pastoring, not the whole.

Self-definition is the issue. My concern is not as much about what name lay pastors carry, it is more about their self-perception. If we believe these people are gifted and called by God to be members of the pastoral team, does not *lay pastor* say that most clearly? A bigger term challenges people to fill it, just as parents buy larger size garments for their children to grow into.

"The name of a business can spell the difference between success and failure. That's why it's critical to choose your name carefully," writes small business columnist Jane Applegate. "Choose a name that reflects your business," she concluded.[10] What name best reflects the business of pastoral care by laypeople?

More churches using our Lay Pastors Ministry model do not use the name *lay pastors* than churches that do. We do not try to control anything churches do with this ministry, including what they call their people. We recommend that they get to know the principles and either use the model as is, modify it or build their own to fit their context.

It's at this point ministry leaders choose a different name. And that's okay as long as choosing another name does not dilute the kind of pastoral care God wants for His people.

I would like to make a case for calling people *lay pastors* so that even if they know themselves as shepherds, lay ministers or care partners (these can all be appropriate designations), they will know what God has called them to be and do.

My case for calling them lay pastors has four points:

1. The lay pastor's care is the same as all members would like to receive from their ordained pastors if there were enough of him or her to go around—P A C E. People would like to have their pastors *pray* for them, their families, their needs and problems daily. They would like their pastors to be *available* (on call), *contact* them by personal visit or phone, know how they are doing, affirm them, inquire about their children, etc. They want to know that they are special in the minds of their pastors, that their pastors remember them. They need an *example* of one who lives close to God, giving himself or herself in service. This is pastoral care. Laypeople are doing it. Shouldn't their name reflect what they do?

2. Laity are called by God to tend the flock, "be shepherds of God's flock." They are partners with the vocational pastors in carrying out this charge. What constitutes tending? Think of a shepherd tending sheep. Tending is being with, listening attentively, loving, being concerned about, nurturing and protecting. These acts translate into pastoring

well. Laypeople are doing these things for microcongrega-
tions of 5 to 10 households.

3. The New Testament Greek word translated "pastor" is
poimane (pronounced poy-main'). It means herdsman or
shepherd. The words of the small business columnist
quoted earlier apply: "Choose a name that reflects your
business." Tending the flock is the lay pastor's business.

4. *Lay* means non-ordained; it does not mean non-gifted or
non-called. The word is from *laos*, as we saw before, which
means *the people of God*. Therefore the name, *lay pastor*, is
appropriate. It is an oxymoron only to those who: (a) do
not understand fully what *lay* and *pastor* mean; (b) have a
difficult time believing laypeople are given spiritual gifts
for ministry as well as clergy; and (c) do not believe
laypeople are called by the same Lord to do ministry.

I rest my case. Having made it, I need to say again, because I am
aware that in some denominations and some churches the name *lay
pastor* is not the wisest choice, my concern is that people know who
they are, and understand what God calls them to do. Choose the name
wisely because a name makes a lot of difference in how people think
of themselves and in how they are received.

Once a name is selected and used, it is almost impossible to change
it and seldom wise to try. Churches starting the ministry will want to
determine specifically what they will ask their people to do and select
the name that most adequately says that. A rose (if it is truly a rose)
called by any other name still smells the same; and a lay pastor (if he
or she is truly a lay pastor) called by any other name still ministers the
same.

I have given three reasons why laypeople can pastor: God gives the
ministry to them; the church gives the ministry to them; and they have
the passion and skills.

"He who has an ear, let him hear what the Spirit says to the churches." Laypeople can give pastoral care: Let them do it!

Notes:

1. These are the real names of real people, all members of Hope Presbyterian Church. They gave permission to be identified by name.

2. See appendix E for the graph that includes January 1994 through March 1996. (Permission given by James H. Hook.)

3. Stephen Ministries, 8016 Dale, St. Louis, Mo. 63117-1449; BeFriender Ministry, 2260 Summit Avenue, St. Paul, MN 55105-1094; People's Ministries, 2704 Old Point Drive, Richmond, VA 23233. There are several others. Siang-Yang Tan, director of the Doctor of Psychology program and associate professor in the Graduate School of Psychology at Fuller Theological Seminary in Pasadena, California, has listed several lay pastoral care ministries in his book, *Lay Counseling: Equipping Christians for a Helping Ministry*. It is published by Zondervan Publishing House, Grand Rapids, Michigan. He includes my book, *Can the Pastor Do It Alone?* (p. 79), and a lengthy description of the Lay Pastors Ministry (p. 199).

4. Paul Stevens and Phil Collins, *The Equipping Pastor* (Washington, D.C.: The Alban Institute, 1993) p. 76.

5. Robert Slocum, *Maximize Your Ministry* (Colorado Springs, Colo.: Navpress, 1990) pp. 7,8.

6. James Garlow, *Partners in Ministry* (Kansas City, Mo.: Beacon Hill Press, 1981) pp. 72-78.

7. Kenneth C. Haugk, *Christian Caregiving* (Minneapolis, Minn.: Augsburg, 1984) p. 19.

8. John Patton, *Pastoral Care in Context* (Louisville, Ky.: Westminster/John Knox Press, 1993) pp. 6,32-36.

9. Thomas F. Taylor, J.D., executive director of the Institute for Ministry, Law and Ethics, a minister in the Presbyterian Church, U.S.A., and author of *Seven Deadly Lawsuits: How Ministers Can Avoid Litigation* (Abingdon) wrote in the January 6, 1997 issue of *Christianity Today*: "How about a large group of lawyers gathered to discuss the best way to sue clergy and churches? In 1992 the American Bar Association hosted just such a seminar, and similar ones have been held regionally throughout the country since then. What is disturbing about these meetings is not their intention of bringing those clergy or churches that act illegally to justice—wrongdoers should be held responsible—but their emphasis is oftentimes on how to land large settlement amounts. A Christian lawyer who attended one such meeting described it as 'blood being poured into shark-infested waters.'"

10. *St. Paul Pioneer Press*, St. Paul, Minn., (September 23, 1989).

PART III:
What Kind of Effort Does It Take?

How to Give Ministry to the People

A TOWER TO BUILD, A BATTLE TO WIN

Desert Hope Wesleyan Church in Phoenix, Arizona, broke the 200 attendance barrier for the first time in its 69-year history only after beginning the Lay Pastors Ministry. It is an exciting story.

From its start in 1926 until 1986, the church seldom averaged more than 65 people in attendance at Sunday worship. The present pastor, Paul Gilbert, was installed on its sixtieth anniversary.

Within three years, the attendance grew to an average of 140. For the next four years, in spite of trying everything Pastor Paul Gilbert and the congregation knew to do, they were never able to break the 200 attendance barrier. Many new people came, but eventually left.

Then they adopted the Lay Pastors Ministry. During the first year of training and commissioning lay pastors, they passed the 200 mark. The church grew by nearly 100 people in one year. This was in 1995 and they are continuing to grow.

Pastor Gilbert draws two substantial conclusions from this experience:

1. A church cannot grow past its ability to care for people; and
2. The pastoral care through laypeople had a causal effect upon the growth.

This historical adventure excited me as I read about it in his Doctor of Ministry dissertation during the days I was writing chapter 1 of this book.[1]

A major reason members are available at Desert Hope and other churches to be trained and deployed into ministry is that laypeople want a significant piece of the action in their churches. It's a new day in the Church. When Betty Moore was executive director of Presbyterians for Renewal, she made this observation:

> In the past, Presbyterians loved the wonderful stories of what God was doing around the world, but today's Presbyterians are hands-on people. They want to participate. There's something exciting about...making mistakes, correcting them, learning...that whole growth process just seems to release an excitement and a dedication.[2]

This is not a new phenomenon; it is a return to how things were done in the formative years of the Christian Church. Jesus gave His ministry to the disciples. When he prayed, "I have brought you [God] glory on earth by completing the work you gave me to do" (John 17:4), He was only 33 years old. He had carried His ministry as far as He should before passing it on to those He was discipling. It was time, not only because He was about to leave the scene, but...just because it was time.

This was not an unplanned handover; it was a planned strategy. He had introduced them to doing ministry without Him earlier by sending them out on their own. He had prepared them by teaching about the Holy Spirit who would enable them to do even greater things than they saw Him do.

Paul did this with Timothy and then instructed him to pass it on to others who were "reliable and qualified" people (2 Tim. 2:2). It's a divine process...passing the ministry on to the people. This is what we did in Cincinnati in 1978. This is what Desert Hope Church did in 1995, and hundreds of other churches—large, medium and small—have been doing. And it continues.

I asked a 12-year-old boy in Hawaii how he learned to play the ukulele so well: "Did you have lessons?"

His reply, "Just by lookin' on," is what we are going to be doing for the next few pages.

This is the way we're going to learn how to give the ministry to the people...just by lookin' on. We're going to look over Paul Gilbert's shoulder in Phoenix to see how he, as pastor of the church, gave the hands-on, grassroots, frontline pastoral care to his people. He provides us with a model that, except for some specifics, parallels many churches I have had a chance to observe or help through the years.

Their adventure starts with an idea: lay pastors providing pastoral care. A leadership team was formed a year before starting the Lay Pastors Ministry to consider that model as a viable option. Their goal was to find the way to grow larger and yet keep the intimacy and warmth of Desert Hope.

Gilbert preached the biblical truths regarding lay ministry. We need to note, at this point, that it was the larger truth of *lay ministry* he taught. Lay ministry is the all-inclusive, full range of ministries carried on by a church. The term can be compared to, shall we say, *sports*. That generic term includes baseball, swimming, golf, soccer, marathon running and other sports. Selecting swimming out of the long list is the same as selecting *lay pastoring* out of a list that includes teaching, missions, youth work, leading worship, administration and more.

Nine months before the first Lay Pastors Institute in which some members would be equipped to be pastors, Gilbert began to preach specifically about the concept of lay pastors being trained and commissioned to actually provide pastoral care.

Six weeks before the Institute, he added the truth that God's desire for His flock was that they be shepherded. In those messages, the concept that a church cannot grow beyond its ability to care for people was introduced. The traditional paradigm, that only the paid professional can minister, was challenged. His preaching began to mobilize those with pastoral kinds of spiritual gifts. He summoned them to do "something great for God." He appealed to them not to put the whole burden on the shoulders of their pastor.

Simultaneously, six weeks prior to the Institute, he began to identify people he believed to have the spiritual maturity and gifts to serve as lay pastors. He personally recruited them. He told them of both the cost and the reward. Most of those he personally contacted seemed eager to receive training in their gift areas.

Paul Gilbert's report reads, "Many showed up to be trained and the congregation as a whole received it well." The Lay Pastors Ministry was under way. He was giving it to the people. Haven't we learned a lot "just by lookin' on!"

IN THE LARGE CHURCH...

In large churches, the procedure is much more complex. What Desert Hope did—focus on the launching of one ministry for several months—is not possible in larger congregations.

Let's look briefly at how a 7,000-member church—the Frazer Memorial United Methodist Church in Montgomery, Alabama—started its lay pastoral care ministry. Earl Andrews, pastor for Congregational Care, had the idea of laypeople doing pastoral care. At that time he discovered my book. Reading it, he realized how his vision could become reality.

He wanted to share his vision with the staff of the church and the 100-member administrative board, so he invited me to tell the story of the Lay Pastors Ministry. A few months later Andrews invited me to conduct a seminar for 35 select people on how to start the ministry. Frazer Memorial's staff eventually customized their own ministry by adapting our model.

They equipped a sizable group of lay ministers (the name they chose for their lay pastors); assigned flocks to them; and had pulpit support by the senior pastor on the Sunday they launched the ministry. The pastor used P A C E for his sermon outline. They added a "point person," Marie Parma, to their staff to manage the ministry, and gave the ministry of pastoral care to the people.

They did it so well that in 1997, 10 years later, the ministry is still flourishing. It is being passed on to other churches through the lay ministry workshops that are offered twice a year in Frazer's popular Church Growth Seminars. As a result of this church's success with these seminars, Marie Parma and some of her people are often invited to assist other churches in starting their lay pastoral care ministries.

The dynamics observed while "lookin' on" at both Desert Hope and Frazer are the same even though a great difference exists in their sizes. Identifying these seven principles will be extremely valuable to church leaders (volunteer or vocational) who either have or are beginning to receive the vision for giving pastoral care or any other ministry to the people. Specific references will be to the Desert Hope Church only because more readers will identify with smaller churches than larger.

Vision: Someone saw possibilities in laypeople doing pastoral ministry and began to share that idea.

Ownership: A leadership team believed in the vision. They considered the Lay Pastors Ministry model and brain-stormed ideas and goals. The pastor's "total involvement" will ultimately segue to "passive involvement" so he can give the same leadership to other yet-to-be-started ministries.[3] A leadership team will need to continue to "own" the ministry as long as it exists.

Enculturation: The culture of the church needs to be seriously considered. By *culture* we mean paradigm, perception or belief pattern that is assumed to always be true. Unless the ministry fits into the culture, the ministry is doomed from the start. Gilbert bravely confronted the traditional paradigm that controls many churches—that only ordained clergy can pastor. His months of preaching the biblical teachings about lay ministry and lay pastoral care made the Lay Pastors Ministry acceptable to the congregation, motivated those with pastoral gifts to step forward and in other ways changed the culture of the church.[4] Note his schedule: intentional preaching started at the nine-month mark and shifted at the six-week mark.

Need: There was a felt need to grow, but also the belief that it is not possible to grow beyond the number for which care can be provided. The heavy burden on the pastor had to find other shoulders.

Structure: They adopted the Lay Pastors Ministry model, persuaded that it would work in their church. They added to some parts and modified others to fit their congregation's needs. The ministry was ready to go when the first people were equipped and commissioned. They had planned the equipping curriculum, set policy for assigning people and provided for the ongoing management of the ministry.

Mobilization: The pastor set the stage for this in his preaching and began making the appeal. He personally selected people and approached them individually. (Moses was instructed to select people with certain qualifications in starting his plan to care for all of God's people under his care, see Exod. 18:21).

Management: Although not mentioned previously, maintenance requirements include office work, flock updating, recruitment, supervision, celebration and evaluation. Frazer added a staff person to manage its ministry.

> **Think of the Lay Pastors Ministry as a tower to build and a battle to win.**

Consider the cost of giving the ministry to the people, and consider your ability to do it. These are the points of Jesus' two parables about building a tower and a king going to war (see Luke 14:28-32). The tower builder was to consider the cost to determine whether he had enough resources to finish what he started; the king was to consider whether he was able to win. Think of the Lay Pastors Ministry as a tower to build and a battle to win. You will want to consider these six points:

1. Consider to whom you are giving the ministry. Laypeople are not volunteers; they are ministers.[5] Granted, people are more familiar with the word *volunteer* and the concept of *volunteerism* than they are with *minister* and *ministry*. These labels are the vocabulary of our secular culture. My wife, for example, was a hospital volunteer for several years, delivering mail and flowers to patients. Everybody understands that terminology and concept.

However, we Christians do not participate only in the secular culture; we have a priority commitment to our Christian culture. The "politically correct" terms and concepts in our Christian culture are *minister* and *ministry*. Our vocabulary and understanding are to be formed by Scripture, not by secular culture. The fact that God sees us as *ministers* doing *ministry* indicates that He puts far more value on us than secular culture does. He, the Creator, calls us to work with Him, and He gives us His Spirit to guide and empower us in accomplishing the tasks He assigns. Consider that you are giving the ministry to the *laos*, God's servant people.

2. *Consider setting process goals as well as an arrival goal.* An example from the early American westward movement helps us understand this consideration and do something with it. The arrival goal was Oregon. The process goals were securing wagons and horses; providing basic supplies such as water, food and fire; coping with sickness and injuries; and confronting the Indians. The preacher must consider that people do not move from a good sermon about lay ministry to doing ministry. The arrival goal of doing ministry is necessary, but it must incorporate many process goals. One major process goal is the formation of a leadership team.[6]

3. *Consider the many barriers.* We can't anticipate all of them, but we can cite a few: Clergy who won't let it happen and laypeople who won't accept it; clergy who do not know how to give the ministry to the people; endorsing the principle, but not proceeding with actions. Matching antidotes are: The paradigm shift; learning from others what was not taught in seminary; and leading in action, not just theology.

4. *Consider that it takes time, patience and perseverance.* I have the following clipping, but I do not know its source:

> The person who looks for quick results in seed planting will be disappointed. If I want potatoes for dinner tomorrow, it will do me little good to go out and plant potatoes in my garden tonight. There are long stretches of darkness and invisibility and silence that separate planting and reaping. During the stretches of waiting, there is cultivating and weeding and nurturing and planting still other seeds.

That takes care of *time*. *Patience* is one of the fruits of the Spirit listed in Galatians 5. God counsels us from Hebrews 12 about *perseverance*: "Let us run with perseverance the race marked out for us" (v. 1). These are significant considerations.

Since my first book gives the specific action steps to take in giving the ministry to the people, I'll not repeat them in this book. However, I have included an updated list in appendix H.[7]

5. Consider what you are giving. It is pastoral care. The Lay Pastors Ministry, or any other lay pastoral model, is a system of congregational care by laypeople. The traditional system for congregational care has been the pastor. That system is not working. The new system is.

6. Consider passing this ministry on, not down. The way pastors perceive ministry will be the way people will perceive it. Many clergy will require a complete paradigm shift to pass it *on* rather than *down*. Unless laypeople also undergo a paradigm shift, the pastor can pass it *on*, but the people will perceive it as being passed *down*.

"He who has an ear, let him hear what the Spirit says to the churches." Ministry belongs to the people: Find a way to give it to them!

Notes:
1. Paul A. Gilbert, "A Strategy for Equipping the Laity for Pastoral Care in the Wesleyan Church," (1996), available from Dr. Gilbert, Desert Hope Church, 2600 North 59th Avenue, Phoenix, AZ 85035.
2. *reNews*, published by Presbyterians for Renewal, 8134 New LaGrange Road, Suite 227, Louisville, KY, (May 1994).
3. For a complete teaching about active and passive involvement, see *The Equipping Pastor* by Paul Stevens and Phil Collins, The Alban Institute, Washington, D.C.; (1993) pp. 64-69.
4. See appendix F for "The New Mind-Set Versus the Old."
5. For a list of differences between volunteer and minister, see the section titled "One Who Is Ready to Obey and Serve" in chapter 10.
6. See appendix G for "Forming the Ministry Leadership Group."
7. See appendix H for "Take This Path."

How This Ministry Fits in Your Church

ONE PIECE OF THE PUZZLE

Two years after moving into our new home in Apple Valley, Minnesota, we began to think about adding another room. We met with the builder to see how it would fit—fit on the lot, fit the architectural design and fit our needs.

The room was built. It fits on the lot perfectly, fits both our exterior and interior designs and fits our needs. It has become the most-used room in our house.

Your congregation has been built. You begin to think about the need for more pastoral care. You meet with The Builder, the one who said, "I will build my church" (Matt. 16:18). You discover what looks like a workable model, the Lay Pastors Ministry.

Questions arise:

- How will it fit in the total life of the church?
- Is there room for it among the organizations and programs?
- Does the need for pastoral care warrant it?
- Will it fit our long-range plan?
- How does it compare with small groups?
- How is it different from the Stephen Ministries model?

If you intend to have a lay pastoral care ministry, it will have to "fit." A "misfit" is a disappointing eyesore, whether it's an added room or an added ministry.

Many questions need to be answered and many factors must be considered. We'll take them one by one in this final chapter. Then, if you see that it will fit and if The Builder will build it, you can proceed with confidence.[1] If this ministry has already been added to your church and you are having problems with the fit, it's not too late to do some remodeling.

THE RIGHT TIME FOR THE RIGHT MINISTRY

The first consideration is timing. Is this the time to start the ministry? The need does not determine the time, because the need is always present.

Timing is essential in the plan of God and the readiness of a congregation. If the builder had suggested adding a room before we were ready, my wife and I would not have been interested. If he had tried to press us, we would have walked away. The need was present from the beginning, but just as with the need for a lay pastoral care ministry, we had to see it ourselves.

The timing must be right. The two churches I wrote about earlier knew it was time to start the ministry.[2] The First Congregational Church in Cannon Falls, Minnesota, realized *the time* had come from the groups that met to identify needs and set priorities. Once they knew, they did not delay.

The Desert Hope Church in Phoenix, Arizona, knew *the time* was now because of its strong desire to grow. The congregation's readiness peaked at the end of a nine-month enculturation period. They started the ministry.

The prototype for the Lay Pastors Ministry developed by College Hill Presbyterian Church in Cincinnati, Ohio, took three sequential periods of time:

1. The need for more pastoral care indicated *the time* had come to get a ministry group together to pray, study and determine what could be done. The group invested 18 months developing the ministry.

2. *The time* had come to launch a pilot project to see if the ministry would work. This took six months.
3. The success of the pilot project indicated that *the time* had come to launch the ministry full scale. We did not delay.

COMPLETING THE PASTORAL CARE PUZZLE

The second consideration must be other kinds of pastoral care happening in the church. The Lay Pastors Ministry may be the major pastoral care effort in one church and the minor one in another. Whichever it is, the ministry has to fit into the total picture like one piece of a jigsaw puzzle has its place in the whole. To do this, the group responsible for the ministry will need to identify the other kinds of pastoring to see where this piece fits.

In some churches, the pastor may be the only other source of pastoral care. In this church there are only two pieces of the pastoral care puzzle, the pastor and the Lay Pastors Ministry. But even the two must be positioned to complement each other so they neither overlap nor create gaps.

Most churches will find many pieces: small groups, organizations, and program departments such as Christian Education or Family Life. Three criteria determine whether pastoral care is happening in groups, organizations and departments:

*   **Sharing:** People are encouraged to share their needs and have an opportunity to be prayed for sometime during every meeting. I know churches where this is a regular part of choir rehearsals, board meetings and planning meetings.
*   **Accountability:** Persons participating know one another so well that if one is missing or facing difficulties, at least one other person will notice and contact them.
*   **Bonding:** They mutually share concerns about spiritual growth, health and relationships.

Fitting a lay pastoral care ministry into this picture requires compiling lists of people receiving pastoral care from other sources. Lay pastors are *not* assigned to them. Someone will have to update these lists regularly because people will be moving in and out of the groups. When a person leaves a group, the pastoral care ministry must pick them up or they will "fall through the cracks."

RECOGNIZING REALISTIC GOALS

The third consideration is your goal. At Hope Church, the Ministry Leadership Group set the goal of providing pastoral care for every household. After a couple of years, the group did a reality check. The church consisted of 1,100 households. The flow of members into the ministry indicated that the goal was unrealistic; all these households would not have lay pastors in any foreseeable future.

With this new insight, the Ministry Leadership Group accepted the challenge to fit the Lay Pastors Ministry into the new picture by changing the goal. The group would now be responsible to *assure* (rather than *provide*) every household that it would receive pastoral care in some form.

They began by identifying those who were cared for in small groups, organizations and program departments. They acknowledged pastoral care from other sources to be adequate and did not assign those people to a lay pastor. Their highest priority was "fringe people," those who were not active in any organization or ministry, and perhaps not even participating in church activities or worship. Now their goal was realistic. The ministry could fit.

LAY PASTORS MINISTRY
AND/OR STEPHEN MINISTRY

The fourth consideration emerges from an often-asked question: "What is the difference between the Lay Pastors Ministry (LPM) and the Stephen Ministry (SM)?"[3]

For some churches, the question is, How does the Lay Pastors Ministry fit in a church which has the Stephen Ministry? or, How does the Stephen Ministry fit in a church that has the Lay Pastors Ministry? Leaders of both organizations are good friends. They believe God has raised up both ministries and that the two complement each other rather than compete.

I see the differences to be:

1. SCOPE:	LPM: A system of congregational care that includes all members of a church on a continuing basis.
	SM: A system of congregational care that gives attention primarily to members who are experiencing difficulties.
2. DESIGN:	LPM: Adaptable to each church's needs and culture; can be started by following the steps in appendix H of this book. (My book, *Can the Pastor Do It Alone?* gives an in-depth look at this process.)
	SM: Requires a prescribed structure and training. Materials available only to enrolled churches.
3. DURATION:	LPM: Continues through good times and bad times. The strategy is to build a long-lasting relationship.
	SM: Lasts through the crisis, then the ministering person is available to be reassigned.
4. QUANTUM:	LPM: One lay pastor cares for 5 to 10 households.
	SM: One Stephen Minister cares for one person.
5. ORIENTATION:	LPM: Relational and spiritual within a Christian bond.
	SM: Relational, spiritual and psychological within a Christian association.
6. TRAINING:	LPM: Ten to 15 hours prepare lay pastors to be "love with skin on it."
	SM: Fifty hours prepare Stephen Ministers with skills to care for troubled people.

Notice their commonalities. Both the Lay Pastors Ministry and the Stephen Ministry...

- Recognize, develop and utilize the giftedness of people;
- Generate an atmosphere of loving and caring within the congregation;
- Require training, support and accountability;
- Utilize similar skills, which include: listening, assertiveness, problem ownership, professionalism, confidentiality and the use of "traditional resources" (prayer, Scripture, witness and blessing);
- Benefit the church: Pastors are released from "overload"; they can sleep at night knowing their people are being cared for. Laypeople feel fulfilled using their gifts, time, energy and faith to make a difference in the lives of others.

The two ministries complement each other; some churches have both. In churches that have both the Lay Pastors Ministry and the Stephen Ministry, Stephen Ministers are resource people for lay pastors who have individuals in their flock encountering crises. Those in crisis will have a lay pastor *and* a Stephen Minister for a period of time. Lay pastors are resource people for Stephen Ministers to give continuing pastoral care when the crisis has passed.

Many churches, after examining both, opt for one or the other, depending upon their priorities, finances and people-potential. The ideal situation is to have both ministries. Together, they provide quite complete grassroots pastoral care coverage.

SMALL GROUP MINISTRY

A big consideration is how the Lay Pastors Ministry fits with small groups. Many organizations are assisting churches in starting, growing, resourcing and sustaining small group ministries. Some churches have a staff person responsible for administrating a Small Group Ministry.

Small groups, where they work, are an effective form of pastoral care; that is, if they include a time of sharing personal needs and joys, followed by prayer for one another about the specifics shared.

Small groups have fared well in some churches. David Trawick, senior pastor of Northwest Hills United Methodist Church in San Antonio, Texas, tells about his church's small group ministry—some are Bible study groups, some support, some recovery. They are based on common interests and life situations. Hear him:

> These small groups do a terrific job of teaching people to minister to each other, rather than to assume it is the pastor's job. My pastoral care load has dropped noticeably since we developed this ministry, because people are truly taking responsibility for the ministry of Christ. Our dream is to increase the number of groups and participants until the entire congregation is involved.[4]

There is always the other side of the coin, however. The February 7, 1994 issue of *Christianity Today* focused on "The Small-Group Takeover." It reports that all is not positive about the movement, and that according to research specialist George Barna, the small-group movement may be waning.

Be that as it may—positive, negative or neutral—not all the members of any church will be in small groups. One large 3,000-member church of my acquaintance, though it promoted small groups for years by assigning every member to a group, training leaders, producing great materials and programming one night a week in the church calendar for small group meetings, still had only 65 percent of its people active in groups. What can a church do about caring for the people who will not or cannot be in small groups?

First, the church must be realistic. Some people cannot be in small groups because of their work schedules, busy agendas, family responsibilities or traveling. Some will not because of their personalities, threatened feelings, spiritual immaturity or indifference.

Coaxing or trying to press people into a small-group mold is not the loving thing to do. The loving thing is to provide another form of pastoral care for them, as did the previously mentioned large church. They invited us to lead them in starting the Lay Pastors Ministry for the 35 percent who were not active in a group. The lay pastors were selected from active small group participants.

With a little creativity, some discussion with concerned people and a lot of prayer, ways can be found to combine a variety of pastoral care forms. The goal for all of us is to fulfill the Great Charter to assure that every household is adequately pastored.

chapter thirteen

EVERY MEMBER COUNTS

Consider next how the Lay Pastors Ministry fits the whole church family. It fits by being elastic enough to stretch around every last one so no one is without personal care and love.

> The Lay Pastors Ministry cannot rest until every last member of the church family is loved and pastored by someone who truly cares.

Jesus' parable of the one lost sheep stretches the pastoral boundary to include even the straying one. Just as the shepherd could not rest until every last sheep was enfolded, the Lay Pastors Ministry cannot rest until every last member of the church family is loved and pastored by someone who truly cares.

This means that everybody counts. The love and care boundary is not allowed to gerrymander, including only "the new and the neat" (as one church was accused of doing) while forgetting the drop-outs, the unresponsive and other not-so-neat people.

Imagine your church to be a solar system. There are those at the center, the committed. Beyond those are the partially committed. Farther

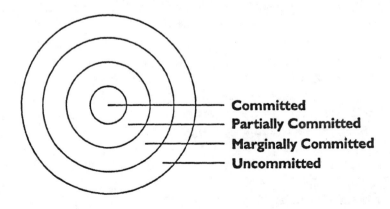

out are the marginally committed; most distant from the center are the uncommitted. Whether at the center or most distant away, each one is precious to the Lord and precious to the Lay Pastors Ministry.

Some garments are touted, "One size fits all." That label belongs on this ministry. The reason it fits all is that lay pastors are providing what all people need: love. All need someone who cares enough to hear them and remember them. Every last one, even the wandering ones, need someone to P A C E them (Pray for them, be Available to them, Contact them and be an Example). One ministry fits all.

LOVE REQUIRES TOUGH PEOPLE FOR PEOPLE TOUGH TO LOVE

The Lay Pastors Ministry requires tough people. It's easy to care for those we like and those who like us, but what about the others? Jesus makes it tough for us. Listen to Him:

> If you love those who love you, what reward will you get? Are not even the tax collectors doing that? And if you greet only your brothers, what are you doing more than others? Do not even the pagans do that? (Matt. 5:46,47).

True love is tough. Have you ever wondered how Jesus must have felt in His humanity? He was misunderstood, sentenced to death by crucifixion in a kangaroo court, spit on, cursed and nailed to the cross while fully alert. And, in spite of the cruelty, He prayed from the cross a prayer of love: "Father, forgive them" (Luke 23:34). Love is tough! This ministry is carried on by people who have that kind of love. That's why this ministry fits all the people in the church family.

One of our lay pastors was assigned an elderly man who had not been in church since his wife died. "His wife had the religion." He had joined years before only to please her. Even though he had professed faith in Jesus Christ as his Savior and Lord when he joined (it is not possible to join a Presbyterian church without affirming this personal faith), that faith had obviously never taken root in his heart. He was not very interested in having a lay pastor, especially one who talked about his faith and wanted to pray with him.

It took a long time, but the lay pastor's love melted his resistance. He finally prayed to receive Christ. His profession and possession were now congruent. It is a point of interest that one of his first acts after this experience was to write a generous check to the church. He was catapulted from the farthest distance in our imaginary solar system to the center. Love is tough. It kept the lay pastor P A C E-ing this man through many difficult and discouraging months. While not much else fit this man, love did. This ministry fits all.

It fits Generation X, thirty-something people, baby boomers, people who are slow to adapt to Christian morals because they didn't grow up in a Christian environment, the biblically illiterate, those who have divorced, those with AIDS, the handicapped, the unconventional, people of all races, the confined, the senile and all others who have become a part of your church family. This ministry fits all because it takes the *all* of Galatians 3:26-28 seriously:

> You are *all* sons of God through faith in Christ Jesus, for *all* of you who were baptized into Christ have clothed yourself with Christ. There is neither Jew nor Greek, slave nor free, male nor female, for you are *all* one in Christ Jesus (italics mine).

THE LARGE PICTURE

Another crucial consideration is how the ministry fits into the large picture—the whole purpose of the church, the witness of its people between Sundays, and the church's participation in the kingdom of God.

Because the Lay Pastors Ministry is the organized and visible caring initiative within the church, it raises the caring quotient of the whole congregation. When a church of 500 members, for example, has 20 to 40 people who intentionally love and care for others, the spirit of the whole church is enriched.

Love and care spreads like the yeast a woman mixed into the flour until "it worked all through the dough" (Luke 13:21). This ministry mixes love and care into the lives of people until it works through all the church.

The Church, being a model of the kingdom of God, is to be attractive to people not yet in the Kingdom. Jesus said, "By this all men [and women] will know that you are my disciples, if you love one another" (John 13:35). And we sing, "They will know we are Christians by our love." By seeing that God's people have genuine and enduring love, people will be drawn to His kingdom.

"He who has an ear, let him hear what the Spirit says to the churches." *Let laypeople do it!*

Notes:

1. Matthew 16:18. My belief is that the Lord is using the Lay Pastors Ministry as one way of building His Church.
2. See chapter 1 for the Cannon Falls, Minnesota, church and chapter 12 for the Phoenix, Arizona, church.
3. Stephen Ministries, 8016 Dale, St. Louis, MO 63117-1449.
4. *Net Results*, "Building A 'High-Touch' Church," vol. XVI, no. 8, (August 1995): 4, Herb Miller, Editor, 5001 Avenue N, Lubbock, TX 79412-2993.

APPENDICES

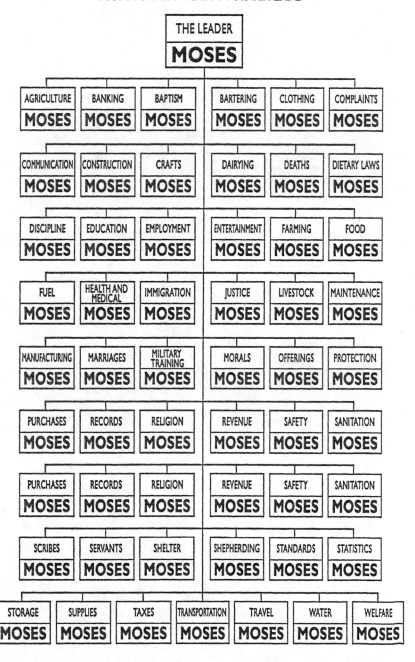

appendix A

MINISTRY CENTRALIZED

THE LEADER
MOSES

AGRICULTURE **MOSES**	BANKING **MOSES**	BAPTISM **MOSES**	BARTERING **MOSES**	CLOTHING **MOSES**	COMPLAINTS **MOSES**
COMMUNICATION **MOSES**	CONSTRUCTION **MOSES**	CRAFTS **MOSES**	DAIRYING **MOSES**	DEATHS **MOSES**	DIETARY LAWS **MOSES**
DISCIPLINE **MOSES**	EDUCATION **MOSES**	EMPLOYMENT **MOSES**	ENTERTAINMENT **MOSES**	FARMING **MOSES**	FOOD **MOSES**
FUEL **MOSES**	HEALTH AND MEDICAL **MOSES**	IMMIGRATION **MOSES**	JUSTICE **MOSES**	LIVESTOCK **MOSES**	MAINTENANCE **MOSES**
MANUFACTURING **MOSES**	MARRIAGES **MOSES**	MILITARY TRAINING **MOSES**	MORALS **MOSES**	OFFERINGS **MOSES**	PROTECTION **MOSES**
PURCHASES **MOSES**	RECORDS **MOSES**	RELIGION **MOSES**	REVENUE **MOSES**	SAFETY **MOSES**	SANITATION **MOSES**
PURCHASES **MOSES**	RECORDS **MOSES**	RELIGION **MOSES**	REVENUE **MOSES**	SAFETY **MOSES**	SANITATION **MOSES**
SCRIBES **MOSES**	SERVANTS **MOSES**	SHELTER **MOSES**	SHEPHERDING **MOSES**	STANDARDS **MOSES**	STATISTICS **MOSES**

STORAGE **MOSES**	SUPPLIES **MOSES**	TAXES **MOSES**	TRANSPORTATION **MOSES**	TRAVEL **MOSES**	WATER **MOSES**	WELFARE **MOSES**

MINISTRY DECENTRALIZED

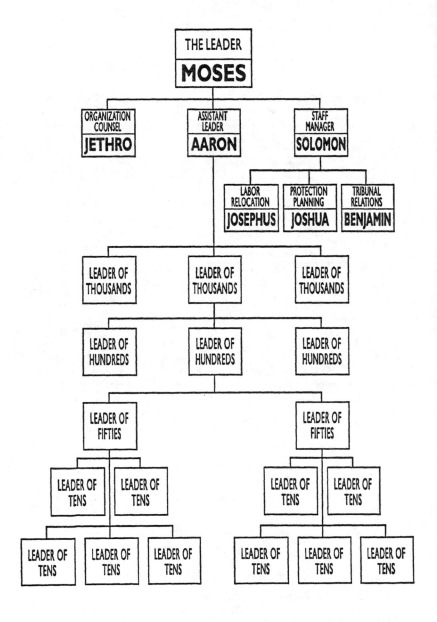

LAB I

Determine where your church is in relation to the following seven qualities. Locate your church on each continuum. This can be done by any group, committee or board. Individuals can do this to find out where they themselves are in their thinking and growth.

Circle the appropriate number. It is best not to take too much time pondering. Your first impulsive diagnosis is probably the most correct.

	Not At All									100 %
Needs-Conscious	1	2	3	4	5	6	7	8	9	10
Gift-Oriented	1	2	3	4	5	6	7	8	9	10
Mobilized	1	2	3	4	5	6	7	8	9	10
Ministry-Balanced	1	2	3	4	5	6	7	8	9	10
Egalitarian	1	2	3	4	5	6	7	8	9	10
Biblical	1	2	3	4	5	6	7	8	9	10
Failure-Resistant	1	2	3	4	5	6	7	8	9	10

After calculating the group's average for each line, circle the number on another photocopied form. This number should approximate where your church is. Now that you have an idea of where your church is, you can do something to make it stronger.

The plan: organize task forces, committees or action groups, one for each quality to (1) articulate their concerns, (2) pray about the quality, (3) strategize and (4) lead the church in developing these qualities.

When I was pastor of Westminster Presbyterian Church in Duluth, Minnesota, we had 10 committees working on 10 different uses for a new church building. These uses included music, youth, Sunday School, finances, architecture, worship and others. If this process worked well for building a building, can't it also work well for building the members? Of course! Go to it!

LAB 2

PASTORS' AUTHORITY AND ACCOUNTABILITY

I watched the pilot of a Boeing 737 taking authority and being accountable one day. I was waiting for my flight, looking out the window at this man walking around the outside of his plane, examining the motors, kicking the wheels, looking up at the underside of the fuselage and wings. I learned that this was standard procedure. Why? He was soon to take the plane and its occupants into the sky. He was in authority.

He was also accountable—to the people in the cabin, to the company, to his family and to himself. He was flying a plane he had neither made nor serviced; he was making certain it was airworthy. He carried people who were dependent upon him to reach their destination safely. He was working for a company whose image was dependent upon his performance. He was responsible to his wife and children to return home safely.

Questions to discuss:

1. How does the pilot's authority and accountability parallel that of the pastor of a church?
2. Who built the church and services it?
3. How is the pastor responsible for the success of the church's mission?
4. What is the nature of the pastor's authority?
5. What is the extent of the pastor's authority?
6. To whom is the pastor accountable?

appendix D

LAB 3

SIX STEPS FOR DISCOVERING
WHAT GOD WANTS ME TO DO

Step 1: Open myself to God as a channel for His use. (Circle one)

closed   partially closed   partially open   open

Step 2: Examine my aspirations for Christ in service. (What I would do in my church if I had my choice.) Write three works of service I would do if I could choose.

1.
2.
3.

Step 3: Identify the needs I believe to be the most important in the life of my church.

1.
2.
3.

Step 4: Evaluate the results of my efforts to serve. (List all forms of service.)

Service:_____

(circle one)   failure   so-so   effective

Service:_____

(circle one)   failure   so-so   effective

Step 5: Follow the guidance of the Holy Spirit as He leads me into obedience to Christ. To the best I am able to know my mind and heart (thoughts and feelings), it seems that God wants me to do this or these work(s) of service:

1.
2.

Step 6: Remain alert to the responses of other Christians. After talking with others about step 5, I believe I should: (check one)

Commit myself to do the following:
1.
2.

Think and pray seriously about doing the following:
1
2.

appendix E

SAINT JOHN'S PASTORAL CARE RECORD

TOTAL MONTHLY LAY MINISTRY CONTACTS REPORT DATE: JANUARY 5, 1997						
Month/Year	Home Visit	Other Visit	Phone	Mail	Other	Total
January 1994	29	84	97	14	15	239
February 1994	19	73	69	42	13	216
March 1994	17	82	59	65	26	249
April 1994	20	67	78	34	14	213
May 1994	22	92	58	17	13	202
June 1994	22	92	49	14	12	189
July 1994	14	71	54	23	6	168
August 1994	14	63	82	27	16	202
September 1994	24	82	74	9	8	197
October 1994	20	71	48	33	16	188
November 1994	15	58	65	66	15	219
December 1994	47	61	50	86	23	267
January 1995	18	85	53	6	14	176
February 1995	11	81	57	65	8	222
March 1995	12	103	59	19	9	202
April 1995	13	111	52	61	17	254
May 1995	16	76	80	40	27	239
June 1995	19	88	62	16	19	204
July 1995	21	94	131	16	17	279
August 1995	20	80	105	24	17	246
September 1995	18	78	74	29	24	223
October 1995	17	106	68	36	25	252
November 1995	18	96	60	72	20	266
December 1995	48	100	57	78	24	307
January 1996	21	85	90	20	8	224
February 1996	17	110	107	64	26	324
March 1996	11	92	41	23	18	185
April 1996	16	72	63	52	25	228
May 1996	11	74	71	22	28	206
June 1996	14	95	45	19	32	205
July 1996	17	64	60	29	20	190
August 1996	17	91	52	16	10	186
September 1996	19	94	69	17	24	223
October 1996	13	106	63	30	25	237
November 1996	33	59	43	52	15	202
December 1996						

appendix e

Months (1994, 1995, 1996)

▬▬ Total Contacts

appendix F

THE NEW MIND-SET VERSUS THE OLD

Old: The pastor is called by God to be a minister.
New: Every Christian is called by God to be a minister.

Old: Ministry is the task of the pastor, supported by the people.
New: Ministry is the task of the people, supported by the pastor.

Old: The people assist the pastors in doing what they believe God is calling the pastor to do.
New: The pastors assist the people in doing what they believe God is calling the people to do.

Old: The pastor has all of the gifts required to nurture and care for a congregation.
New: All of the people together have the gifts required to nurture and care for a congregation.

Old: The pastors bear the burden of the ministry. The people hold the pastors up in prayer.
New: Both people and pastors bear the burden of the ministry. They hold one another up in prayer.

Old: The pastor is accountable to God and the members for doing the ministry. Laypeople who serve are accountable to the pastor.
New: All Christians are ministers and are accountable to God and the church leaders.

Old: Seminaries are to educate and train certain "called" people for the ministry.
New: The church is to educate and train the members to be ministers.

FORMING THE MINISTRY LEADERSHIP GROUP

I. Know Your People
a. As you share your vision, log the names of the people who are possibilities. Consult other staff members, church leaders or those who seem to be in tune with your vision. Ask about people they would suggest.
b. Note that Jesus had hundreds of people from whom to choose.
c. As much as possible, select a variety of people in gifts, personality, relationships and experience.

II. Draft Qualifications
Moses, the apostles and Paul had qualifications for leaders (see Exod. 18:14-27; Acts 6:1-6; 1 Tim. 3:1-13).

a. Committed: To Christ and the church; also, able to commit themselves to a group.
b. Mature: Shall have proven themselves in faith and in ministry.
c. Available: Not overly committed to other ministry or activities. Does his or her life situation permit time, energy and sustained attention to this ministry?
d. Creative: Capable of combining traditional methods and forms with emerging principles to create a new ministry. Imaginative. Flexible to release their holds on previous methods and accept the new.
e. Communicative: Ready and willing to talk—can express themselves bravely and clearly. Neither aggressive nor passive, but assertive in handling competitive ideas and proposals. Can verbalize abstractions and concepts.

III. Pray
Jesus prayed all night about His list (see Luke 6:12-16). Trust God to lead those of you involved in the selection process.

IV. Contact

    a. Send letters telling those who have been selected to be a member of the Lay Pastors Ministry Leadership Group. Share the vision with them. Ask them to pray about it. Tell them that you will phone to arrange a time when you can meet with them to talk and pray about their acceptance.

    b. At your meeting:
- Share your vision.
- Explain the purpose of the Ministry Leadership Group.
- Clarify goals, expectations and commitments.
- Pray together about their responses.

V. Number

A large number is not required. Use your "person power" in the hands-on ministry. For a smaller church, 3 to 5 people are sufficient; for larger churches, 5 to 12. You will be able to determine your ideal number as you develop the various areas of the ministry.

VI. Responsibilities

Eight tasks are essential. Each one may be done by one individual. Smaller churches will want to assign the eight tasks to 3 or 4 people. The tasks: Ministry Leadership Group leader; ministry leader; secretary; communications; calling forth (enlisting); equipping: koinonia (fellowship); and evaluation. For the full description of each of the eight tasks—we call the document a "Position Accountability Write-Up"—contact Lay Pastors Ministry, Inc., 7132 Portland Avenue South, Minneapolis, MN 55423. Phone: 612-866-4055 ext.54; Fax 612-423-9245.

TAKE THIS PATH:
IT LEADS TO A LAY PASTORAL CARE MINISTRY

Five Key Assumptions
1. There is a need for this ministry.
2. God calls the Church to meet the need.
3. Laypeople can give pastoral care.
4. Church members will accept pastoral care from peers.
5. A small group will commit themselves to ownership of the ministry.

Six Big Steps
1. *Share* the vision.
   a. God calls us to "Tend the flock" (1 Pet. 5:1-4, *RSV*).
   b. Identify the need for pastoral care in your church, and sort through your thoughts and feelings about it.
   c. Share the vision with:
      * Potential ministry leadership group members
      * Official church board
      * Congregation

2. *Organize* a ministry leadership group.
   a. Draft qualifications:
      * Committed
      * Mature
      * Available
      * Creative
      * Communicative
   b. Agenda should include five parts:
      * Log in (sharing how things are in each one's life)
      * Worship
      * Nurture
      * Ministry development and management
      * Fellowship
   c. Adopt a collegial leadership style.

3. *Design* the ministry structure.
   a. Lay the foundation. (the Twelve Foundation Blocks)
      - Vision
      - Ownership
      - Design
      - Call
      - Equipping
      - Accountability
      - Affirmation
      - Support
      - Fellowship
      - Communication
      - Evaluation
      - Maintenance
   b. Determine how the ministry fits into your total church life.
   c. Determine what your lay pastors will do.
      - P A C E: *Pray* for each one regularly, be *Available, Contact* regularly, provide a Christian *Example*
      - Frequency of contact
      - Commitments:
        1. To Christ and the church
        2. To continue being equipped
        3. To accountability
        4. To meeting together regularly
   d. Decide what you will call your pastoring people.
   e. Establish the process.
      - Call forth prospective lay pastors.
      - Determine the content of equipping.
      - Set time and place for equipping.
      - Confirm the call of each applicant.
      - Assign flocks.
      - Prepare ministry items: brochures, report forms, cards, etc.
      - Set times for lay pastors to come together regularly.
   f. Plan for ministry maintenance.

4. *Secure* official board approval.

5. *Prepare* the congregation.
   a. Preach and teach lay ministry.
   b. Inculcate the following basic beliefs:
      - Every member is a minister, gifted and called.
      - Mutual ministry characterizes the Christian community.
      - Vocational ministers are called to equip the volunteer ministers (Eph. 4:11,12).
      - Being equipped is essential to ministry.
      - Refer to Scriptures: 1 Corinthians 12:1-7,11; 1 Peter 5:1-4; Romans 12:4-8, Exodus 18 (The Mosaic model).

6. *Call* people into ministry. Do what you designed: *Let laypeople do it!*